Practice Management for Paralegals

Michelle Roy McSpurren
Rebecca Bromwich

 emond ▪ Toronto, Canada ▪ 2018

Emond Montgomery Publications Limited
60 Shaftesbury Avenue
Toronto ON M4T 1A3
http://www.emond.ca/highered

Printed in Canada.
Reprinted September 2020.

We acknowledge the financial support of the Government of Canada.   Canadä

All quotations from the *Paralegal Professional Conduct Guidelines*, *Paralegal Rules of Conduct*, and *By-Laws*: Copyright 2012, The Law Society of Upper Canada. Reproduced with the permission of the Law Society of Upper Canada.

Vice president, publishing: Anthony Rezek
Publisher: Lindsay Sutherland
Director, development and production: Kelly Dickson
Developmental editor: Joanne Sutherland
Production editor: Natalie Berchem
Copy editors: David Handelsman, Rose Knecht
Permissions editor: Alison Lloyd-Baker
Typesetter: Tom Dart
Text designer: Tara Agnerian
Proofreader: Marg Anne Morrison
Indexer: David Gargaro
Cover image: Marie C. Fields/Shutterstock

Library and Archives Canada Cataloguing in Publication

Roy McSpurren, Michelle, author
    Practice management for paralegals / Michelle Roy McSpurren, Rebecca Bromwich.

Includes bibliographical references and index.
ISBN 978-1-77255-006-1 (softcover)

    1. Legal assistants—Canada.   2. New business enterprises—Canada.   I. Bromwich, Rebecca, author   II. Title.

KF320.L4M37 2017   340.023'71   C2017-903547-9

To the students I have had the pleasure to teach and to learn from, to my teenaged daughter who actually *wants* to come to work with me on "Take Our Kids to Work Day," and to my parents and my husband who love and support me in everything I do. To the memory of my lovely grandmother who was so proud of me when I became a full-time professor two months before she passed away.

—MRM

For all of those, in all fields of legal services, working hard to provide access to justice.

—RB

Brief Contents

Detailed Contents

1 Introduction and Overview

2 Methods of Starting a Business

3 Regulatory and Legal Issues When Starting Up

4 Planning for Start-Up

5 Maintaining Your Business

6 Clients and the Public

7 Practice Management

8 File Management and Time Management

Preface

In its previous edition, this text was called *Small Business and Practice Management for Paralegals.* With the publication of this new edition, the title has been changed to *Practice Management for Paralegals.* This textbook is designed to assist paralegal students in understanding key aspects of running a paralegal practice. Some of you may intend to open your own practice once you have worked in the profession for a few years; some of you may never intend to do so, but find that your intentions change over time. Even if you never open your own paralegal practice, the information in this textbook will assist you in complying with your obligations as a practising paralegal.

As you are likely aware, paralegals in Ontario are governed by the Law Society of Upper Canada. The Law Society of Upper Canada has created the *Paralegal Rules of Conduct, Paralegal Professional Conduct Guidelines,* and various By-Laws which, together, set standards for paralegals. Recently there have been significant changes to the Rules and Guidelines governing marketing and advertising by licensees, referral fees, and fee splitting. This textbook discusses those changes, as well as the proposed expansion of paralegals' scope of practice to include certain family law matters as recommended in the document that has come to be known as the "Bonkalo report" (the Family Legal Services Review Report). The text has been much expanded and now includes a feature contributed by a practising paralegal entitled "Planning for Practice," as well as a sample retainer agreement, file opening checklist, and scenarios that enable students to consider the applications and confirm their understanding of the Rules and Guidelines.

The textbook also discusses case law concerning the legal doctrine of privilege as it pertains to paralegals, accounting and record-keeping obligations, misleading advertising, and competence.

Chapter 1 of the text provides an introduction and overview to the topic of running a paralegal practice and allows the reader to conduct an entrepreneurial self-assessment to determine whether he or she is suited to running a paralegal practice. Chapter 2 discusses methods of starting a business and addresses the potential need to "moonlight" while waiting for a new practice to become profitable. Chapter 3 discusses business structures which may be used by paralegals who start their own practices as well as other legal and regulatory issues affecting such a business.

Chapter 4 emphasizes the importance of planning, market analysis, and financial planning, and provides a sample business plan for a fictional paralegal business. Chapter 5 discusses the recent changes to the Rules and Guidelines concerning marketing, advertising, referral fees, and fee splitting. In addition, that chapter discusses hiring employees and client retention strategies.

The paralegal–client relationship is the focus of Chapter 6, which discusses the paralegals' professional obligation to be competent, to maintain client confidentiality, to avoid conflicts of interest, and to maintain errors and omissions insurance. The chapter also identifies situations in which it is appropriate for a paralegal to withdraw from representation, and contains a sample non-engagement letter as well as a sample retainer agreement.

In Chapters 7 and 8, the focus changes to financial obligations, the duty to care for client property, delegation of tasks to staff, file management, and time management.

It has been seven years since the publication of the first edition of this text and in that time there have been many changes to the Rules, Guidelines, and By-Laws governing paralegals. This edition of the textbook focuses on those changes that directly affect paralegals who plan to open their own practices, but it is important that all licensed paralegals—employees and entrepreneurs—be aware of these ethical obligations.

Acknowledgments

I would like to acknowledge that without Rebecca Bromwich this book would not exist. Although it has been renamed, this is the second edition of her text. Rebecca provided valuable feedback on chapters as the writing of this text progressed and it was she who gave the book its structure. I would also like to acknowledge the valuable contributions of Duane Booth, a licensed paralegal who has his own practice. Duane prepared the Planning for Practice scenarios and provided precedent documents tailored to the textbook. I owe him thanks for patiently awaiting my revisions to the text and promptly submitting his scenarios for the revised chapters.

Special thanks to my colleagues at Sheridan for their assistance as I prepared this edition of the textbook. I relied heavily upon Professor Patricia Knight's textbook *Ethics and Professional Practice for Paralegals*, 3rd edition, as well as upon the materials Professor Gargi Mukherji culled and prepared for Sheridan's course on paralegal practice management. I owe a huge thank you to Professor Netta Romano, who very kindly switched vacation periods with me so that I could have the summer off to move house and to finish the revisions to this textbook.

I would also like to thank the reviewers of the text: Lesley Wagner, Durham College; Stacey Pipicelli, Fanshawe College; and Rosemarie Ortiz, Mohawk College, as well as the staff at Emond: Lindsay Sutherland for waiting to sign me up as co-author until I had time to work on this project, Kelly Dickson for seamlessly transitioning me from one editor to another, Joanne Sutherland for her patience, Natalie Berchem for her work on the galleys, and Rosalind Wright for always getting me out of a jam when I need instructor copies of textbooks in a hurry. I would also like to thank Rose Knecht for her wonderful copyediting.

—Michelle Roy McSpurren

I would like to acknowledge the support and mentorship of my PhD thesis committee and my other colleagues at Carleton University's Department of Law and Legal Studies. Also, always, thank you to my husband for his unwavering support and my children for the energy they bring to my everyday.

—Rebecca Bromwich

About the Authors

Michelle Roy McSpurren is a full-time professor in the Faculty of Applied Health and Community Studies at Sheridan College. Professor Roy McSpurren has taught a variety of legal subjects to paralegal, law clerk, business, accounting, and marketing students at various colleges. She has over ten years of teaching experience and has been teaching at Sheridan College for seven years. Professor Roy McSpurren currently teaches in the Paralegal Program at Sheridan College, in addition to acting as Academic Advisor in that program.

Professor Roy McSpurren holds an LLB degree from Osgoode Hall Law School and is a member of the Ontario Bar. She obtained her MA from York University, specializing in English. Her BA (Hons) degree, conferred by that same university, emphasized creative writing in addition to English.

Professor Roy McSpurren's areas of academic interest include legal writing, legal research, paralegal practice management, torts, contracts, and business law. She regularly teaches courses in all these areas. Prior to teaching, Professor Roy McSpurren worked in legal publishing for several years and has edited and contributed to journals, newsletters, and other publications in the areas of contracts, torts, education law, condominium law, corporate law, and business law.

Rebecca Jaremko Bromwich has been an Ontario lawyer for over 16 years. She worked in private practice from 2003 to 2009, starting at a large firm, doing a wide range of litigation work. She also worked for six years as Staff Lawyer, Law Reform and Equality, to the Canadian Bar Association, then as a Policy Counsel with the Federation of Law Societies of Canada. Now, she is Program Director for Carleton University's Graduate Diploma in Conflict Resolution program. Dr Bromwich is also an Assistant Crown Attorney with the Ministry of the Attorney General in Ottawa. She is a member of the Alternative Dispute Resolution Institute of Ontario (ADRIO) and has a certificate from the Program on Negotiation Master Class at Harvard University (2017).

Rebecca received her PhD in 2015 from Carleton University's Department of Law and Legal Studies, and was the first ever graduate of that program. She was awarded a Carleton Senate Medal as well as the 2015 CLSA Graduate Student Essay Prize for her graduate work. Rebecca also has an LLM and LLB, received from Queen's University in 2002 and 2001 respectively, and holds a graduate certificate in Women's Studies from the University of Cincinnati.

In addition to her several years teaching at the University of Ottawa's Faculty of Law, Rebecca has taught at the University of Western Ontario's Faculty of Law, and at the University of Cincinnati. She has also been a columnist for The Lawyers Weekly and has authored and co-authored several legal textbooks for students and legal system practitioners, including lawyers, paralegals and police.

Introduction and Overview

1

LEARNING OUTCOMES

After completing this chapter, you should be able to:

- Explain the Law Society of Upper Canada's role in regulating paralegals in Ontario.

- Recognize certain traits required to be a successful entrepreneur.

- Describe the factors to consider when deciding whether or not to start your own paralegal business.

Entrepreneurship, Innovation, and Work as a Paralegal

If you are reading this textbook, then you are likely enrolled in a program that has been accredited by the **Law Society of Upper Canada (LSUC)** to provide you with the education you need to become a duly licensed paralegal. Whether you have just embarked upon that education or whether you are well into that education, it is important for you to understand the role of the LSUC in regulating paralegals in Ontario. Key information about the role of the LSUC and its expectations of paralegals is provided in legislation, by-laws, rules, and guidelines governing paralegals in Ontario.

The LSUC defines a **paralegal** as a person who provides legal services. Paralegals are members of the LSUC (*Law Society Act*,[1] ss 1(1) and 2(2)(d)) and, as such, are governed by the LSUC. The LSUC grants licences to individuals who are qualified to work as paralegals, and establishes licensee requirements (By-Law 4, ss 8(1) and 13(1)). The LSUC can impose sanctions on those who do not comply with its rules and regulations—for example, by revoking their licences or fining them.

Legal services are defined as "conduct that involves the application of legal principles and legal judgment with regard to the circumstances or objectives of a person" (*Law Society Act*, s 1(5)). The LSUC's *Paralegal Rules of Conduct*[2] outline the scope of the services that paralegals are allowed to provide in Ontario, as well as specific rules regarding how they are to provide those services. See Chapter 6 for a further discussion of paralegals' scope of practice. Legal services that fall outside of the regulated scope of what paralegals are permitted to do can only be performed by lawyers.

As previously stated, the LSUC is a professional organization that governs legal services in Ontario. Its mandate is to protect the public by ensuring that the people of Ontario are served by lawyers and paralegals who meet appropriately high standards of education, competence, and conduct. Founded in 1797 to allow lawyers to govern their colleagues' conduct and protect the public, the LSUC has regulated lawyers for centuries.

In 2007, the LSUC began licensing and regulating paralegals with the aim of providing the people of Ontario with more choice and protection and improved access to justice. The LSUC's decision to do so made Ontario the first province to license paralegals and regulate the profession. Paralegals who practise in Ontario have obligations to their clients, to the general public, and to the administration of justice; prospective licensees must demonstrate to the LSUC that they have experience providing legal services, pass a licence examination, pay fees, and meet other requirements relating to good character and training (By-Law 4, ss 8(1) and 13(1)).

Unlike law clerks, who must work under the supervision of a lawyer, paralegals can operate private practices. Regardless of how proficient a paralegal is with respect to legal matters, the success of his or her practice will depend to a large extent on

---

1   RSO 1990, c L.8, as amended.

2   Law Society of Upper Canada, *Paralegal Rules of Conduct* (1 October 2014; amendments current to 2017), online: <https://www.lsuc.on.ca/paralegal-conduct-rules>.

efficient and effective business management. Effective advertising and marketing, client management, accounting systems, bill collection, insurance, and staff supervision are important factors contributing to success.

Paralegals must always observe the professional obligations imposed on them by the LSUC. In addition to handling matters in the above areas effectively, paralegals preparing to start their own business must be aware of limitations on their conduct and the nature of their work, and must keep their professional knowledge current.

Improper behaviour by legal professionals can have potentially devastating consequences for both clients and members of the public. Refer to the LSUC's *Paralegal Rules of Conduct* ("the Rules") and the *Paralegal Professional Conduct Guidelines* ("the Guidelines"),[3] which can be found on the Law Society's website at <http://www.lsuc.on.ca/paralegal-conduct-guidelines>. It is important to consult both the Rules and any guidelines interpreting those Rules. It is both of these documents together that set out most of the LSUC's expectations of paralegals. Additional information about paralegals' obligations is contained in the By-Laws.[4] Improper behaviour by legal professionals can result in complaints to the LSUC about a paralegal's conduct and in disciplinary action. These disciplinary decisions are made by the Law Society Tribunal. The tribunal's decisions are available to the public on the Canadian Legal Information Institute (CanLII), an electronic database maintained through public funding from law societies across Canada.

Entrepreneurial Self-Assessment

As leaders of small businesses, **entrepreneurs**—those who organize and manage an enterprise, especially a business—are responsible for a high degree of business innovation, often developing new and better ways of doing things. As sole proprietors, or as principals of closely held corporations, they can make decisions and act without the need to convince others of the validity of their ideas or obtain permission beforehand. On the other hand, entrepreneurs assume a high level of personal stress and financial risk. For paralegals, these challenges are amplified by the added responsibilities and obligations of running a small business within a regulated profession, since entrepreneurial initiative must operate within the parameters of the LSUC rules.

> **entrepreneur**
> an individual who starts up a new business

Entrepreneurship involves a particular skill set and range of tasks, as well as considerable risk. While estimates vary, more than half of small businesses fail within the first five years. The success or failure of a small business that provides human services, such as legal services, depends in part on the trade skills of the entrepreneur, but business acumen is also significant.

Not everyone is suited to running a small business, and assessing whether or not becoming an entrepreneur is a good choice for you can be challenging. The following are some personality traits, as well as other factors, to consider.

---

3   Law Society of Upper Canada, *Paralegal Professional Conduct Guidelines* (1 October 2014; amendments current to 2016), online: <http://www.lsuc.on.ca/paralegal-conduct-guidelines>.

4   Law Society of Upper Canada, By-Laws, online: <https://www.lsuc.on.ca/by-laws>.

Initiative

*Things may come to those who wait, but only the
things left by those who hustle.*

—Abraham Lincoln[5]

Above all others, the trait that is generally acknowledged as the most important for entrepreneurs to possess is a willingness to take initiative and get things moving. As their own bosses, entrepreneurs must be self-starters; no one is watching them to ensure that they perform their work. They must be able to avoid the temptation of procrastination.

Prospective entrepreneurs should enjoy taking on leadership roles and should not need to rely on others to provide them with direction. Motivation, self-discipline, and a positive attitude are important prerequisites for entrepreneurial success. The best entrepreneurs often thrive on challenge.

Interpersonal Skills

*To be successful, you have to be able to relate to people; they have to be
satisfied with your personality to be able to do business with you and to
build a relationship with mutual trust.*

—George Ross

The provision of legal services is a particularly people-oriented activity. It is a service industry in which you are selling credibility and trust. The ability to communicate effectively with clients and members of the public face to face, over the telephone, and in writing is an important skill for legal professionals to possess.

Social boldness—for example, the ability to strike up conversations with new people—is another important quality, as you must be able to network, foster new business relationships, and ultimately convince others to buy your services. Are you comfortable cold calling businesses to obtain work? This might include, for example, handling Small Claims Court collection and enforcement files. While many times a cold call will result in the sound of a dial tone, if you do not even pick up the phone to make a call, you have already lost that potential client. You will also require social confidence and negotiation skills when dealing with opposing counsel on behalf of your clients. In a 2015 CIBC World Markets article, "Secrets to Small Business Success," attracting and retaining clients was identified as a key factor in the success of small businesses.[6]

The ability to network with colleagues and mentors is also useful. Entrepreneurs who seek out and rely on expert advice from senior colleagues and professionals are much more likely to see their business revenues increase than those who do not. This may also be a source of referrals. Mentors and colleagues are particularly important resources for paralegals who intend to practise alone. Organizations such as the

---

5 Lincoln was a lawyer before he became president of the United States.
6 CIBC World Markets, "Secrets to Small Business Success" (April 2015), online: <https://www
.cibc.com/ca/pdf/sb-secrets-for-success-en-v1.pdf>.

Paralegal Society of Canada, Ontario Paralegal Association, and Women's Paralegal Association of Ontario may offer reduced or free memberships for students. If you intend to open your own paralegal firm one day, remember that it is never too early to begin networking.

Entrepreneurial paralegals must also employ their interpersonal skills in dealing with suppliers, such as document servers and couriers. Those with larger operations may require staff, and management skills will be important.

Calculated Risk-Taking

Often the difference between a successful person and a failure is not one has better abilities or ideas, but the courage that one has to bet on one's ideas, to take a calculated risk—and to act.

—André Malraux

When opening their small businesses, entrepreneurs assume many forms of risk—for example, in deciding who to hire, where to locate, where to advertise, and whether or not to take on particular business partners or clients.

People who are risk-averse—those who prefer to "play it safe" and stay within the existing frameworks of their jobs—are probably not ready to take on the responsibility of entrepreneurship. On the other hand, those who are too willing to take risks may act recklessly and endanger their businesses.

The best entrepreneurs are those who assess situations carefully and then determine whether or not particular risks are worth taking, basing their decisions on a reasoned assessment of the possible consequences of different courses of action.

Decisiveness

If I had to sum up in a word what makes a good manager, I'd say decisiveness. You can use the fanciest computers to gather the numbers, but in the end you have to set a timetable and act.

—Lee Iacocca

Entrepreneurs are their own bosses. If you like clear structure and directions before and during a task and constructive feedback upon completing it, you are probably more suited to working as an employee than running your own business. Similarly, if it is difficult for you to decide on a course of action—whether because you tend to act rashly, without considering alternatives, or because you have trouble making up your mind—you may not be suited to being your own boss. To self-assess, it might be helpful to consider an example of decision-making from your personal life. Picture yourself at a restaurant that you are visiting for the first time. How long does it typically take you to order from the menu? Do you read the whole menu? Do you change your mind several times before ordering? Are you the last person at the table to order? Do you decide too quickly and regret your choice? Are you likely to default to that ordering style when running a business?

People who make good entrepreneurs are confident, enjoy making considered decisions, and like being in charge. They must be sufficiently decisive to make decisions independently and to deal with the consequences of those decisions sensibly.

Planning and Skills

Good fortune is what happens when opportunity meets planning.

—Thomas Alva Edison

Because they are responsible for planning where their businesses should go in the future, entrepreneurs must be able to make both short- and long-term plans. In order to do so, they must be organized and must take responsibility for seeing tasks through to their conclusions. As discussed under the heading "Flexibility," entrepreneurs must also be willing to adapt their plans in order to adjust to changes in circumstances when required. Planning that is too rigid may leave no room for creativity or flexibility.

Specialized education and/or training can be important to an entrepreneur's success. Innovation, Science and Economic Development Canada's *Key Small Business Statistics* report, published in 2016, looked at statistics concerning the educational levels of small business owners and found that the highest concentration (30.8 percent) fell in the college, CEGEP, or trade school diploma category.[7] Figure 1.1 shows the highest level of education attained by small and medium enterprise owners in 2014. Taking the time to acquire business knowledge and skills—in addition to professional knowledge and skills particular to paralegals—through continuing education, self-study, and work experience will increase your chances of success.

Flexibility

Stay committed to your decisions, but stay flexible in your approach.

—Tom Robbins

Entrepreneurs are commonly viewed as people who are very responsive to change and who have the ability to perceive opportunities that others may not see. Because there is no "boss" to consult or convince beforehand, entrepreneurs are often in a position to make decisions quickly, which can allow them to benefit from new opportunities as they present themselves. For example, a paralegal who sets up a business with the intention of defending traffic tickets for clients may be wise to reconsider if offered a sizable contract to do debt collection work.

While advance planning is crucial for success, equally crucial is your ability to "keep your ear to the ground" without losing sight of overall goals, and a willingness to modify your business plan as circumstances change.

---

7   Innovation, Science and Economic Development Canada, *Key Small Business Statistics* (June 2016), online: <https://www.ic.gc.ca/eic/site/061.nsf/vwapj/KSBS-PSRPE_June-Juin_2016_eng .pdf/$FILE/KSBS-PSRPE_June-Juin_2016_eng.pdf>.

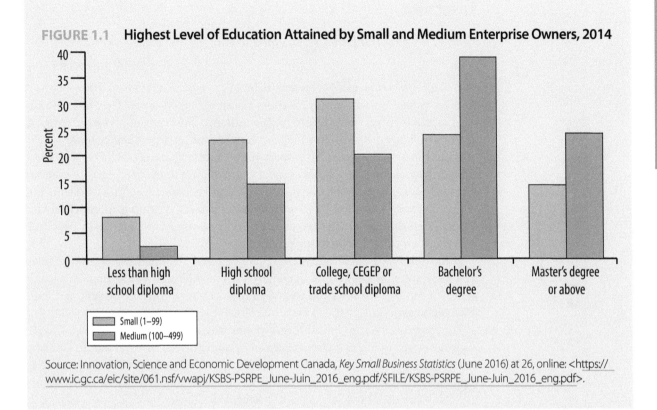

FIGURE 1.1 Highest Level of Education Attained by Small and Medium Enterprise Owners, 2014

Source: Innovation, Science and Economic Development Canada, *Key Small Business Statistics* (June 2016) at 26, online: <https://www.ic.gc.ca/eic/site/061.nsf/vwapj/KSBS-PSRPE_June-Juin_2016_eng.pdf/$FILE/KSBS-PSRPE_June-Juin_2016_eng.pdf>.

Resourcefulness

At the outset of your career as an entrepreneur, you may be a one-person operation. To reduce your start-up and operating costs, you should consider taking on some basic tasks yourself. This might mean painting your office yourself; setting up your own computer, printer, and fax machine; assembling your own furniture; buying your own office supplies; and so on. You will not have an IT department or secretary to rely on, and may have only yourself.

It is also important to determine what you can do yourself and what requires expert assistance. For example, if you intend to do your own bookkeeping, before you purchase accounting software specially designed for legal professionals it may be wise to speak to legal professionals who currently use the software to determine whether it will meet your needs. You may require training in the use of that software. Alternatively, your time might be better spent on marketing initiatives than on painting your office, and you might decide to hire a student to do the painting even if you are capable of doing it yourself. Remember that you are likely to be your highest-paid employee and your time is valuable.

Investment

In any investment, you expect to have fun and make money.

—Michael Jordan

One of the major reasons why it is risky to be an entrepreneur is that, as the saying goes, "it takes money to make money." Starting a business can be expensive. Entrepreneurs need capital to invest toward office rental, insurance, Internet and phone, advertising, and other office expenses before they can earn any money from their business.

Unfortunately, the payoff from operating a small business is often slow to materialize. Entrepreneurs can probably expect to lose money in the first year—or even the first few years—of operating a business. Cash flow shortages are typical. Nonetheless, taking on excessive debt is often what sinks a business. Planning appropriately for expenditures through credit that can realistically be carried and eventually paid back is a crucial aspect of the planning process.[8]

Some fortunate individuals will have money saved. For others, saving money may be a motivation for working as an employee for a while after graduating. This has at least two benefits: it allows you to save money to invest in your business, and it allows you to gain skills that will make your business a safer investment.

For the majority, who must borrow money, having good credit will help. Checking your credit rating and cleaning up any problems may be essential. In Canada, consumers are entitled to obtain free credit reports from the credit rating agencies Equifax and TransUnion Canada. Information on how to order a free credit report is provided by the Financial Consumer Agency of Canada.[9]

A line of credit will supply you with money at a much lower cost than a regular credit card, but it may be difficult to acquire a line of credit without a steady income. If you are employed before you open your own business, you should apply for a line of credit at that time. It may also be necessary to offer security, such as equity in a home. If, like most recent graduates, you do not yet own a home, consider whether you have a relative willing to guarantee your line of credit.

Support Network

A wide support network of family and friends can be instrumental to your success. From such a network you may be able to obtain a financial investment or support from family members, assistance with the start-up process from friends with particular expertise, and/or advice from mentors and colleagues. Strong relationships and numerous contacts can provide you with the emotional, practical, and professional support you will need through the ups and downs of starting up a business. Once you are licensed, that wide network of family and friends may also lead to word of mouth referrals—a key source of clients.

---

8   See, for example, Susan Ward, "Why Do Small Businesses Fail?" online: <https://www.thebalance.com/why-do-small-businesses-fail-2948582>.

9   Financial Consumer Agency of Canada, "Ordering Your Credit Report," online: <https://www.canada.ca/en/financial-consumer-agency/services/credit-reports-score/order-credit-report.html>.

Perseverance

It's not that I'm so smart, it's just that I stay with problems longer.

—Albert Einstein

Although initiative is important for an entrepreneur, people who are only good at starting things—not finishing them—are not cut out to be entrepreneurs. An entrepreneur's business will likely grow slowly, and the ability to follow through despite obstacles is an important key to success. Success as an entrepreneur will be difficult for those who tend to procrastinate or give up when they don't see results quickly.

The responsibility that comes with starting a paralegal business can be overwhelming, and being able to deal productively with the inevitable frustrations—and to find solutions to problems in a calm, level-headed manner—is essential.

For paralegals, sticking with problems until they are solved is not just a wise business practice, but an ethical obligation. A paralegal who enters into a retainer with a client is ethically obligated to continue to represent that client unless withdrawal from representation can be justified in accordance with the Rules (Rule 3.08). Guideline 5, section 1 of the *Paralegal Professional Conduct Guidelines* states:

> 1. One of the most important duties of a paralegal is the duty of service to his or her *client*. This duty includes obligations to be competent, maintain confidentiality, avoid conflicts of interest and continue to represent the client unless the paralegal has good reason for withdrawing.

Guideline 11 describes several relevant factors to be considered prior to withdrawal of representation. Managing client expectations by honestly and fairly discussing the likely risks and costs of clients' matters is important to the business success of paralegal entrepreneurs.

Although some entrepreneurs start their small businesses in part to achieve a better work–life balance—for example, out of a desire to spend more time with their families—many must consistently work long hours to achieve their goals. Seeing tasks through to their conclusions is a process that takes time.

Purpose and Overview

As a student in a legal services program today, you are preparing to begin your career at an exciting moment in the history of the provision of legal services in Ontario. As a licensed paralegal, you will assume and be required to meet significant professional responsibilities, and will have the chance to benefit from historically unrivalled opportunities.

Only those paralegals who practise ethically and professionally, and who gain and apply sound business knowledge, will profit from current, and future, opportunities. It is the hope of the authors that *you* do. The purpose of this book is to allow you to explore and discuss issues that you should consider if you are thinking about starting your own paralegal practice, and to provide you with the basic tools you will need if you decide to do so.

This chapter dealt with small business issues.

Chapter 2 compares the advantages and challenges of starting a new business from scratch with purchasing an existing business.

Chapter 3 explores regulatory and legal issues related to starting a business. It explains the different forms a business may take (including sole proprietorship, partnership, and professional corporation), the obligations of paralegals with respect to compliance with both Canadian and Ontario business laws and regulations and the relevant LSUC rules, and the requirements for registering business names. It also looks at issues regarding taxes, licences, zoning, home offices, and insurance.

Chapter 4 outlines what is involved in planning for the start-up of a business. It discusses customer and market profiling, market analysis, and the development of a marketing plan. It also considers financial analysis (including analysis of start-up costs and cash flow), management plans (including their implementation), and the development of a business plan.

Chapter 5 looks at what is involved in maintaining a small business. Relevant rules—such as those relating to business communications, advertising, and setting fees—are explored. As well, the chapter considers personnel management (including issues relating to the hiring and termination of employees, and setting policies) and client retention strategies.

Chapter 6 considers paralegals' professional obligations when dealing with clients. It discusses retainer agreements and non-engagement letters. It considers the obligations of paralegals with respect to confidentiality and errors and omissions insurance.

Chapter 7 addresses practice management through an exploration of general obligations, professional responsibility, financial responsibilities, bookkeeping and record-keeping, supervisory responsibilities, and delegation.

Chapter 8 focuses on file management. Confidentiality is considered within this context, and management tools and the organization of file contents are discussed. Recommendations are made to help you comply with LSUC rules regarding management of client property, and closing and storage of inactive files. The chapter also deals with appropriate uses of technology. Time management is reviewed within this context, as are checklists and tickler systems, docketing, and communicating with clients.

KEY TERMS

entrepreneur, 3
Law Society of Upper Canada (LSUC), 2
legal services, 2
paralegal, 2

USEFUL URLS

The Balance. "Starting a Business." <https://www
.thebalance.com/starting-a-small-business-4073888>.

Business Development Bank of Canada. "Entrepreneurial
Potential Self-Assessment." <https://www.bdc.ca/en/
articles-tools/entrepreneur-toolkit/business-
assessments/pages/self-assessment-test-your-
entrepreneurial-potential.aspx>.

Law Society of Upper Canada. By-Laws. <https://www
.lsuc.on.ca/by-laws>.

Law Society of Upper Canada. *Paralegal Professional
Conduct Guidelines*. <http://www.lsuc.on.ca/
paralegal-conduct-guidelines>.

Law Society of Upper Canada. *Paralegal Rules of Conduct*.
<https://www.lsuc.on.ca/paralegal-conduct-rules>.

Law Society of Upper Canada. "Resources for Paralegals."
<http://www.lsuc.on.ca/for-paralegals/
resources-for-paralegals>.

Law Society Tribunal Disciplinary Decisions.
<http://www.canlii.org/en/on/onlst>.

Ontario Paralegal Association. <http://www
.ontarioparalegalassociation.com/cpages/homepage>.

Paralegal Society of Canada. <http://pscanada.ca>.

Women's Paralegal Association of Ontario.
<http://www.wpao.ca>.

REVIEW QUESTIONS

1. What is the definition of a "paralegal" in Ontario?

2. What is the LSUC and what is its role with respect to
the paralegal profession?

3. To whom do paralegals have obligations and where
are these obligations described?

4. What are some traits of entrepreneurs? What other
factors should would-be entrepreneurs consider?

5. Where can you find the *Paralegal Rules of Conduct*?

6. Why is it important to read the Guidelines when
reading the *Paralegal Rules of Conduct*?

Methods of Starting a Business

2

LEARNING OUTCOMES

After completing this chapter, you should be able to:

- Compare the advantages and challenges of opening a new business with those of purchasing an existing business.

- Distinguish between purchasing the assets of a business and purchasing a corporation.

- Identify benefits and potential pitfalls of second jobs for paralegals who choose to "moonlight" while starting their own business.

Starting a New Business

There are advantages as well as challenges associated with building a new business from scratch. Doing so involves a great deal of planning, including the development of a comprehensive business plan; the identification of customers, market potential, and start-up costs; and the formulation of financial projections (discussed in Chapter 4). It is also necessary to determine what form the business should take (see Chapter 3).

Although the amount of planning required to do so can seem daunting, and certainly is significant, starting a new business allows entrepreneurs to be inventive and creative, and to make something entirely new. Those who construct their businesses from scratch are free to shape them however they choose, within the scope of the regulatory context and the law. Successful entrepreneurs report great personal satisfaction in knowing that they have developed a business independently, from the ground up.

Another advantage of building a business from scratch may be a lower initial cost; purchasing an existing business will likely involve more early expenditures, or at least more spending all at once.

It may be possible to start a new business on a part-time basis, "moonlighting" from a paying job with another business association and building your commitment to the new business over time. Working a "day job" while you build up your business may be difficult and you must be careful to comply with *Paralegal Rules of Conduct* ("the Rules").[1] Even if your day job is something completely unrelated to the law, Rule 2.01(4) provides that

> (4) [a] paralegal who engages in another profession, business, occupation or other outside interest or who holds public office concurrently with the provision of legal services, shall not allow the outside interest or public office to jeopardize the paralegal's integrity, independence, or competence.

In essence, paralegals cannot allow their other interests (including other jobs) to negatively affect the level of service they provide to their clients when they are working as paralegals. Paralegals must also be careful that they maintain their independence.

Rule 2.01(5) states:

> (5) A paralegal shall not allow involvement in an outside interest or public office to impair the exercise of his or her independent judgment on behalf of a client.

Guideline 2 of the *Paralegal Professional Conduct Guidelines*[2] also has a great deal to say on this subject. Outside interests need not be connected with the provision of legal services, although they may be (for example, teaching in a college's paralegal

---

1 Law Society of Upper Canada, *Paralegal Rules of Conduct* (1 October 2014; amendments current to 2017), online: <https://www.lsuc.on.ca/paralegal-conduct-rules>.

2 Law Society of Upper Canada, *Paralegal Professional Conduct Guidelines* (1 October 2014; amendments current to 2016), online: <http://www.lsuc.on.ca/paralegal-conduct-guidelines>.

program). Section 2 of this guideline is of particular interest. It states that when a paralegal participates in community activities, he or she should be careful about how his or her role is perceived. The paralegal should not

> be involved in any outside interest in such a way that makes it difficult to distinguish in which capacity the paralegal is acting, or that would give rise to a conflict of interest.

If the paralegal believes that the outside interest will impair his or her ability to act in the best interest of his or her client, the paralegal is obliged to either cease representing the client or cease participating in the outside interest (Guideline 2, s 3). Guideline 9, sections 40 and 41 also discuss the potential for conflict arising from the paralegal's outside interests.

Working for someone else in a business similar to the one you wish to start can provide you with valuable knowledge and experience, but you must ensure that you are not competing unfairly or illegally with your employer. The Rules—in particular, those regarding conflicts of interest—impose constraints on what other kinds of work paralegals may take on (Rules 3.04, 3.05, and 3.06; Guidelines 5, 7, and 9). Conflicts of interest are covered in more detail in Chapter 6.

In addition to limits on moonlighting that are imposed by the Rules, the spectre of possible civil liability looms if an employee competes unfairly with his or her employer. An employer can sue an employee in contract and tort for competing unfairly. Restrictive covenants in employment contracts can impose upon employees limits on who they can work for. Further, employees have a general duty of loyalty to their employers, which can be breached if the employees compete unfairly with the employer. Of course, not all outside work is considered unfair competition: employees have a right to earn a livelihood, but work in a competing industry or business raises the prospect of civil liability. See *Elsley v J G Collins Ins Agencies.*[3]

Purchasing an Existing Business

For many entrepreneurs, and especially for paralegals, there are a number of reasons why it may make sense to purchase an existing business rather than to start a new one.

Purchasing an existing business—for example, from a paralegal who is preparing to retire—will usually require less planning than starting from scratch, since much of the planning required for a successful business will already have been done. The market for the services will have been tested and demonstrated. Existing legal services businesses are often sold with their client bases, meaning that a group of clients has already been established (although clients remain free to take their business elsewhere). Income levels for the business will be set and will probably be reasonably predictable.

An existing business will likely have a reputation on which to build. Over time, businesses build up **goodwill**—an intangible asset that can be bought and sold with

goodwill
an intangible asset consisting of a business's reputation and brand, measured by the difference in the value of its assets (minus liabilities) and the market value of the company

---

3   [1978] 2 SCR 916.

the business. A business's goodwill is the difference in the value of its assets (minus liabilities) and the market value of the company. It is the amount, in excess of a business's asset value, that a reasonable purchaser could be expected to pay for the entity as a whole—in other words, it is the value of the business's reputation and brand.

Many existing businesses will have employees who wish to continue working with the organization after the new owner purchases it. Their expertise and experience can help ease the ownership transition, preserving client relationships and the flow of business income.

Despite the advantages outlined above, the decision to buy an existing business should only be made after considerable thought and investigation. Moreover, because of the high initial costs, not everyone will have the option of purchasing an existing business. Significant capital—or at least substantial credit—will be required. Over and above the purchase price, it is also likely that several months' worth of working capital will be required to ensure the business has adequate cash flow.

Any business purchase should include a consideration of whether or not the ability of the previous owner to compete with the purchaser will be limited. For example, if a paralegal sells her business to you, is there a written agreement preventing her from setting up an office next door and soliciting customers away? If so, what is the duration of that agreement and what geographical area is covered by the agreement? What if she sets up her business 10 kilometres away rather than next door? What if she sets up her business in a neighbouring city? The purchase and sale agreement should include provisions for non-competition and non-solicitation of clients. These types of clauses are known as restrictive covenants and must be carefully drafted in order to be enforceable, although the courts are more inclined to enforce these contracts in the context of a sale of a business or business assets. Be prepared to retain a lawyer to draft the purchase and sale agreement.

The sellers of a business will often be willing to give advice to the purchasers. Some sellers will offer this advice for free, especially if the purchase price is paid over time; in this case, the seller will have an interest in seeing that the business succeeds under its new ownership. In other instances, sellers will provide the business advice for a fee, and this consulting arrangement may be included in the purchase and sale agreement.

Remember that buying a business can also affect your legal obligations with respect to reporting of income tax. The Canada Revenue Agency has a great deal of information on this topic. Taxes will be discussed in more detail in Chapter 3.

Rather than buying a business from another paralegal, you may be able to join a partnership of paralegals. This is common practice in law firms. After working at a law firm for a number of years as an employee, a lawyer may be offered the opportunity to become a partner. This model is often adopted by paralegals operating in partnership, as it allows them to gain experience and expertise with a secure paycheque before acquiring an ownership interest.

Due Diligence

The term **due diligence** is used to refer to the investigation of a business, a person, or the performance of an act in accordance with a particular accepted **standard of care**. When considering the purchase of a paralegal business, you are legally

due diligence
investigation of a business or a person, or the performance of an act to ensure compliance with legal or other standards

standard of care
the level of care, competence, or prudence required to avoid liability for negligence

obligated to make reasonable inquiries and investigate the business entity carefully. You should scrutinize the business's legal, financial, staffing, tax, information technology, and market situations. It is also a good idea to consult with the LSUC to determine whether or not there are any outstanding complaints against the practice.

Prospective purchasers should look closely at the business's debts and potential liabilities. **Liabilities** are obligations of persons or entities that arise from past events or transactions—for example, debts or financial obligations. Are there contracts that will involve ongoing obligation or payments that you as the new owner will have to honour? Purchasers should examine finances carefully to determine whether or not there are outstanding debts, and should consider taxes and other obligations to ensure that all payments are up to date. Regulatory and legal compliance issues are also important. Purchasers should investigate whether or not the business is in breach of any law or if there are any pending lawsuits.

It is also wise to consider why the current owner is selling the business. Prospective purchasers should try to find out whether or not the business has been neglected; an anonymous visit in person can provide valuable insight into this question. Because reputation is extremely important to a paralegal's business, you should also consider the business's reputation and whether this will be an advantage or a disadvantage to your operation. To do this, it will be helpful to consult with other professionals in the industry.

Prospective purchasers should consider staffing issues. When a corporation is sold, all employment contracts with the corporation as employer continue to exist, and the new owner becomes responsible for termination pay if he or she chooses to fire anyone. If there are long-term employees that the purchaser does not wish to keep, termination pay can amount to a substantial liability.

In the case of a sale of a **sole proprietorship**—that is, a business owned by a single individual, where there is no legal distinction between the owner of the business and the business itself—all employment contracts are automatically terminated and the seller is responsible for paying termination pay to all employees. This is because the sole proprietor was the employer—only in the case of a corporation is there a separate business entity that continues to employ the same staff. (Forms of business organization will be discussed in more depth in Chapter 3.) Employment contracts may not legally be assigned (or transferred) from the sole proprietor to the purchaser of the business. The seller must therefore pay termination pay to the employees, who may then negotiate new employment agreements with the purchaser.

In much the same way that a business's clients may choose to take their business elsewhere, employees may quit their jobs at any time. A purchaser cannot assume that employees or clients will remain loyal to the business after a transfer of ownership.

Asset Purchase

Determining precisely what is being offered for sale is another important part of assessing the cost of purchasing an existing business. A business's **assets** include items of value that may be tangible, such as buildings or equipment, or intangible, such as

liabilities
debts and other financial obligations

sole proprietorship
a business owned by a single individual, where there is no legal distinction between the owner of the business and the business itself

asset
item of value owned by a company or person, including tangible items such as buildings and equipment, and intangible ones such as telephone numbers and licences

asset sale
a sale in which a business's tangible assets are sold, but not its name, corporate identity, work in progress, and goodwill

business name, goodwill, telephone numbers, or licences. In an **asset sale**, only a business's tangible assets are sold; this does not include the business's name, corporate identity, work in progress, and goodwill. While asset sales are much more common in the manufacturing sector, where there is substantial machinery and equipment to sell, it is still important to be clear on what is being purchased in any business sale. If *only* the assets are purchased, the purchaser will not be obtaining work in progress and goodwill.

If the purchase is an asset sale, the purchase and sale documents should include a detailed account of what assets are being sold. A meticulous list should be made of all of the physical objects—for example, the photocopier, desks, chairs, customer lists, and telephones. Purchasers should think carefully about what the fair value of the assets is—for example, equipment offered for sale may be obsolete and of little value. If you wish to purchase used office equipment and furniture at a discounted price, you may be better off searching online classifieds websites such as Craigslist and Kijiji for the specific items you need.

Price

A potential purchaser of an existing paralegal business should be very careful when negotiating the purchase price, and should consider hiring a professional to help determine what a reasonable value is. An appraiser can provide an estimated fair market value of assets, including any depreciation in the value of equipment or other assets. A business valuator can calculate more complex issues, such as future earning potential.

Conclusion

Paralegals who wish to start businesses as providers of legal services can choose to start their businesses from scratch or decide to purchase an existing business. Both options involve their own unique advantages and challenges. Although starting a business from scratch requires a great deal of planning, it allows entrepreneurs to be inventive and creative, and can be deeply rewarding. On the other hand, while paralegals who purchase an existing business have less planning and uncertainty to deal with and have the business's existing reputation on which to build, not everyone can afford the high initial costs. Prospective buyers should investigate the business very carefully.

Purchasing a corporation in itself is not the same as purchasing that corporation's assets, and potential buyers should find out what exactly is being offered for sale when assessing the costs of purchasing an existing business. When negotiating a purchase price for a corporation and/or its assets, potential purchasers should consider hiring a professional to help them determine what a reasonable value is.

KEY TERMS

asset, 17
asset sale, 18
due diligence, 16
goodwill, 15
liabilities, 17
sole proprietorship, 17
standard of care, 16

USEFUL URLS

Artim, Greg. "Purchasing an Existing Business—Legal Do's and Don'ts." <http://ezinearticles.com/?Purchasing-an-Existing-Business—-Legal-Dos-and-Donts&id=509495>.

Brooks Barristers and Solicitors. "Key Questions and Issues When Purchasing a Business in Canada." <http://canadian-lawyers.ca/Understand-Your-Legal-Issue/Business-Law/Buying-and-Selling-of-Businesses/Key-Questions-and-Issues-When-Purchasing-a-Business-in-Canada.html>.

Canada Revenue Agency. "Buying a Business." <http://www.cra-arc.gc.ca/tx/bsnss/tpcs/lf-vnts/byng/menu-eng.html>.

Law Society of Upper Canada. *Paralegal Professional Conduct Guidelines*. <http://www.lsuc.on.ca/paralegal-conduct-guidelines>.

Law Society of Upper Canada. *Paralegal Rules of Conduct* (2007, as amended). <https://www.lsuc.on.ca/paralegal-conduct-rules>.

REVIEW QUESTIONS

1. Describe some advantages of starting a new business as opposed to taking over an existing one.

2. Describe some advantages of purchasing an existing business.

3. What is goodwill?

4. What is due diligence?

5. What is an asset sale?

SCENARIO-BASED QUESTIONS

1. I Scream You Scream

Johan is a newly licensed paralegal. To put himself through college, he worked as a waiter for Carmel's Catering Ltd. Johan is starting his own practice, and to supplement his income he works weekends for the catering company. The boss of the catering company, Carmel Toscano, wants to retain Johan to commence actions in Small Claims Court against people and companies that have not paid their accounts. Carmel has a terrible temper and often yells at her staff, including Johan.

a. Does Johan's job at Carmel's Catering Ltd. mean that he is not in a position to take on this work?

b. Would your answer to a. change if Johan was so intimidated by his boss, Carmel, that he felt unable to make appropriate settlement recommendations in the face of her anger about the unpaid accounts?

2. The Perfect Job?

Carla Lawson has had some trouble establishing her paralegal practice. To supplement her income, she works part-time at a local college teaching business law to marketing, accounting, and business students. Margo Holt, one of Carla's students, is chatting to Carla on a class break. Margo mentions that her father, a general contractor, wants to hire an in-house paralegal to take on his business's litigation matters. Carla Lawson secures an interview with Mr. Holt and is given the position. Two weeks later Carla begins working for Mr. Holt at Holt Home Renovations. Margo, who is usually an A student, receives only a B+ grade in the course taught by Carla. Margo tells her father to fire Carla, but he refuses to do so. Should Carla resign from her position with Holt Home Renovations to avoid a conflict of interest or for any other reason?

Regulatory and Legal Issues When Starting Up

3

LEARNING OUTCOMES

After completing this chapter, you should be able to:

- Understand different available methods for conducting business as a paralegal in Ontario, including in the form of a sole proprietorship, a general partnership, a limited liability partnership, and a professional corporation.

- Explain the advantages and disadvantages of operating a sole proprietorship, and of conducting business in partnership.

- Describe the difference between a limited liability partnership and a general partnership, and a partnership and an association.

- Explain the advantages and disadvantages of conducting business as part of a professional corporation.

- Identify when registration of a business name is necessary.

- Identify the various licences a business may require.

- Explain the advantages and disadvantages of home offices.

- Understand the importance of insurance for paralegals and know what type of insurance is mandatory.

Business Forms

When starting a business, you will need to decide what form your business will take. You may decide to operate as a sole proprietorship, a partnership, or a professional corporation. It is important to recognize that not all methods of organizing businesses are open to paralegals practising in Ontario. A common form of business organization that is not available to those paralegals is the corporation, although paralegals may organize their businesses as professional corporations. The distinction between corporate forms that matters here will be explained in this chapter. As you will see, each business form has unique advantages and disadvantages. It is also possible to change the form of your business over time. A business that begins as a sole proprietorship may later become a partnership and, still later, could become a professional corporation.

Sole Proprietorship

A sole proprietorship is the simplest form that a business can take. Just as the name suggests, a sole proprietorship is owned and managed by one person. This means that the sole proprietor has the freedom to make decisions that directly affect the business and to manage risks associated with the business. Sole proprietorships are relatively easy to set up and to terminate. The only legal rules for setting up a sole proprietorship involve business name registration and business licensing.

Despite the relatively simple and informal set-up procedures involved, sole proprietorships have their disadvantages—primarily, unlimited personal liability. This is because there is no legal separation between the owner of the business and the business itself. A sole proprietor is personally liable for any debts incurred by the business. This means that paralegals operating as sole proprietors can lose personal assets, such as their cars or homes, and be forced into personal **bankruptcy** if sued successfully or if unable to pay their business debts.[1] The paralegal's inability to pay those debts as they become due is called **insolvency**.[2]

In addition, since there is no legal separation between the business and its owner, events such as the sole proprietor's incapacity or death will result in the dissolution of the sole proprietorship. The personal bankruptcy of a sole proprietor is also likely to result in the dissolution of the sole proprietorship.

Sole proprietors are personally responsible for performing all obligations incurred in the course of the operation of their businesses. In addition, they bear exclusive responsibility for any and all civil or criminal wrongs they commit in the course of operating their businesses, and can be held personally responsible for acts committed by their employees in the course of their work. In addition to the law concerning vicarious liability of employers for the acts of their employees committed in the ordinary course of their work, Rules 8.01(1) and (3) of the *Paralegal Rules of Conduct* ("the Rules")[3] provide that the paralegal is responsible for the business entrusted to him or her by clients and for supervising employees to whom particular tasks have

bankruptcy
a legal process governed by the *Bankruptcy and Insolvency Act* for a person who can no longer pay back debt; the person who owes the debt assigns all assets—with some exceptions—to a Licensed Insolvency Trustee who sells it or uses it to help pay the debt to the creditors

insolvency
the inability of a debtor to pay debt as it is due

---

1 Office of the Superintendent of Bankruptcy Canada, "Definitions," online: <https://ic.gc.ca/eic/site/bsf-osb.nsf/eng/br01467.html>.

2 Jan D Weir & Fran Smyth. *Critical Concepts of Canadian Business Law*, 6th ed (Toronto: Pearson Learning Solutions, 2015).

3 Law Society of Upper Canada, *Paralegal Rules of Conduct* (1 October 2014; amendments current to 2017), online: <https://www.lsuc.on.ca/paralegal-conduct-rules>.

been delegated. Guideline 18 provides more detailed information concerning supervision of staff, and By-Law 7.1 also deals with supervision of staff, as well as students, by licensees. These obligations will be discussed in more detail in Chapter 7. The liabilities of paralegal sole proprietors include (but are not limited to) occupier's liability with respect to any injuries that occur on the premises, such as slip and fall, and professional liability for any harm caused to a client as a result of errors or omissions made by the paralegal or his or her employees.

Consider the issues raised in the following scenario.

PLANNING FOR PRACTICE

Sole Proprietorship

Hank Nolan obtained his paralegal licence in March 2014. He was eager to begin his practice, but with student debt and little start-up funding available, he wanted to do so in the simplest, most economic fashion. He chose to set up shop as a sole proprietorship specializing in landlord and tenant matters. Eventually, as the practice grew, took on additional staff and perhaps more paralegals, he would explore other business structures, such as a professional corporation. But that was down the road.

Rather than choose a business name, which would require registration through a Master Business Licence, he chose to initially operate under his own name.

Nolan opened up a separate chequing account at his bank under his name, registered for a GST number under his name and Social Insurance Number, and signed up for a new telephone and fax line under his name. Everything was under his own name. At tax time, he was required to report all income from his practice on his personal income taxes (though he would also be reporting all of his business expenses).

He knew he would be at risk, but he was quickly up and running and taking on clients, all with little money out of his pocket.

Finding clients and managing cases wasn't as easy as Nolan first anticipated— particularly collecting from clients. Several months passed, and with student loan and car payments to make, he wasn't able to remit the three quarterly HST payments he reported to Canada Revenue Agency. He received a letter from CRA threatening action against him, including placing a lien on his car or garnishment of wages if he did not pay the amounts due.

As a sole proprietor, his assets are not protected in the event CRA or any other creditor obtains judgment against him related to the business.

Knowing the personal risks his business presented to him, Nolan took a number of steps to safeguard his interests as he tried to build his business.

Instead of taking up-front retainers, he opted to bill clients in stages of a matter, invoicing them after each stage was completed. This saved him setting up trust accounts and running the risk of "mixing" his bank accounts. He also chose only to represent landlords in disputes as his previous experience with landlord and tenant matters was that tenants were more difficult to collect from after billing.

Still, these safeguards didn't shield him from what could have been a significant run in with CRA had he not found money to pay the HST he collected from clients to the government.

Knowing your property, your investments, or even your home could potentially be at risk, do you think you would go into business as a sole proprietor?

Partnership

partnership
a form of business in which
two or more persons carry
on business together with
a reasonable expectation
of a profit; also called a
general partnership

A **partnership** (also called a general partnership) is a form of business practice in which two or more persons carry on business together with a reasonable expectation of making a profit. Generally, the partners in a partnership all share in the profits or losses of their endeavour. Like sole proprietorships, partnerships are relatively easy to create and terminate.

Section 2 of the *Partnerships Act*[4] makes it clear that a partnership is considered to exist whenever two or more persons or entities find themselves in a business relationship like the one described above. In many cases, courts have found partnerships to exist even where this was not the intention of the parties involved, or where the parties characterized their relationship as something other than a partnership. Section 3 of the *Partnerships Act* sets out some rules that are to be applied when determining whether a partnership exists. Section 3(3) provides:

> 3. The receipt by a person of a share of the profits of a business is proof, in the absence of evidence to the contrary, that the person is a partner in the business, but the receipt of such a share or payment, contingent on or varying with the profits of a business, does not of itself make him or her a partner in the business.

The sharing of profits, then, is a key factor in determining whether a partnership exists.

The *Partnerships Act* provides rules that, by default, govern the relationship between partners—for example, that all partners are equal. However, partners may create partnership agreements, overriding these rules by making their own agreements about how to carry on their businesses. A partnership agreement might, for example, specify that profits and losses will be distributed among partners unequally (and describe how), or that only some partners have a role in managing the partnership. Changes to a partnership agreement generally require the partners' unanimous consent.

> Anna Baker and Lucas Walker graduated from their paralegal training program the same year. They decided to share office space and bank accounts, and carry on business together. The firm name is Baker and Walker. Anna and Lucas are carrying on business as a partnership.

Like a sole proprietorship, a partnership is a *method* of conducting business but it is not legally a business *entity*—meaning that it has no legal existence apart from the existence of the individual partners. In general, and like sole proprietors, partners in a business bear personal liability for all obligations entered into on behalf of the partnership. Any contracts signed or debts owed by the partnership become *personal obligations* of each partner. Lawsuits may be commenced against the partnership, and any court judgment may be collected from each and all partners personally. This kind of liability, known as **joint and several liability**, is one of the main risks and potential disadvantages of the partnership business form.

joint and several liability
shared liability, such that
all parties are equally liable for the full amount
of the debt or obligation

Like sole proprietors, partners can be held personally responsible for acts committed by their employees in the course of their work. Individual partners bear the same supervisory responsibilities as sole proprietors with respect to delegation of tasks to employees and supervision of those employees.

---

4   RSO 1990, c P.5.

Owing to the lack of legal separation between individual partners and the partnership, partnerships will be dissolved in the event of the death or insolvency of a partner unless the partnership agreement provides for the continuation of the partnership in these circumstances (s 33 of the *Partnerships Act*).

Because of joint and several liability, trust between the partners in a partnership is very important. Partners have a **fiduciary duty** to one another, which requires them to act with honesty and in good faith, protecting each other's interests very carefully.

Some additional advantages of forming partnerships are the access to additional funding or capital as partners "buy in" to the practice, the ability to share responsibility for decision-making and management of the firm, and the ability to consult others before making decisions that will affect the future growth of the firm. The prospect of being able to become a partner in time (often five to seven years) may also attract paralegals to become employees of particular firms.

In addition to the kind of partnership described above, two other types of partnerships exist: limited partnerships and limited liability partnerships. **Limited partnerships**, which are governed by the *Limited Partnerships Act*,[5] allow the partners to limit or restrict liability to only some of the partners. In Ontario, this method of business organization is not available to paralegals who provide legal services to members of the public.

In provinces or territories other than Ontario this form of business may be utilized by paralegals. This may be useful if a partnership is seeking investment by a "silent partner" who will not take an active role in the business.

In order to take advantage of the special rules that apply to limited partners, you must file specific forms and information with the government. Limited partnerships must also be identified as such to the public. Finally, limited partners can forfeit the limits on their liability if they participate in the management of their firms.

The third type of partnership, known as a **limited liability partnership**, is governed by the *Partnerships Act*. Sections 44.1 to 44.4 of that Act specifically address limited liability partnerships. Sections 61.1(1)(b),(c), and (d) of the *Law Society Act*[6] and By-Law 7 operate together to permit paralegals to organize their businesses in this manner. Used by many professionals, the main advantage of these partnerships is that they offer limited liability with respect to the professional negligence of other partners. This means that if one partner is successfully sued for professional negligence, the other partners are *not* jointly and severally liable for the amount of the judgment; only with respect to other types of business debts and obligations, such as non-payment of rent or occupier's liability, are the partners jointly and severally liable. The name of a limited liability partnership must include the words "limited liability partnership" or the abbreviation "LLP." This is to notify members of the public that the partners are not jointly and severally liable for professional negligence. In addition, pursuant to section 44.1 of the *Partnerships Act*, limited liability partnerships must have partnership agreements specifying that the partnership is a limited liability partnership and stating that the *Partnerships Act* governs the agreement.

The Law Society of Upper Canada (LSUC) permits paralegals to operate in limited liability partnerships, and such partnerships are common in the legal services

fiduciary duty
an obligation, with respect to financial matters, to put the interests of the person owed the duty above one's own interests

limited partnership
a type of partnership that restricts liability to only one or some of the partners, as set out in a partnership agreement

limited liability partnership
a partnership of professionals where not all of the partners are liable for the professional negligence of one or some of the partners

---

5 RSO 1990, c L.16.
6 RSO 1990, c L.8, as amended.

industry. By-Law 7 requires that all partners in a limited liability partnership maintain their own professional liability insurance coverage in accordance with By-Law 6.

Each form of business entity has advantages and disadvantages, but liability for others' actions is a key consideration for the paralegals in the following scenario.

PLANNING FOR PRACTICE

Limited Liability Partnership

Carlos Wilson, Angela Watson, and Stanley Clarke graduated together from a paralegal training program in 2010. Each started their paralegal careers in individual practice as sole practitioners. Carlos is highly skilled in small claims litigation and he built up a strong client base in a relatively short time. Angela's strengths are in the accident benefits field and she had built a solid reputation and was receiving a notable increase in referrals. Stanley had worked in-house for a corporation managing provincial offences matters, workplace safety, and employment standards, and was looking to move on to providing legal services to the public.

Two years later the three met for coffee to discuss jointly forming a new paralegal law firm. During their time in school, they found they worked well together and had a strong personal and professional rapport. By combining their individual strengths, they were convinced they had the makings of a successful legal practice.

Joining forces would also be financially beneficial to each paralegal, they determined. Instead of maintaining individual practices and each incurring expenses for office space, bank fees, equipment costs, and office expenses, they would be able to share these resources and be in a position to hire staff to assist them with handling their caseloads effectively and, in turn, provide better service to clients.

Once they agreed on taking the plunge and starting their own firm, the first order of business was determining the form this new firm would take. They briefly explored the possibility of forming a general partnership, where each would be entitled to share equally the profits of the business, but would also jointly take on full liability for each other's negligence. They were not prepared to go that route, particularly since both Carlos and Angela had had previous clients threaten to sue them when those clients did not like the outcome of their matters. Instead, Angela, Carlos, and Stanley opted to form a limited liability partnership.

The three paralegals drafted their partnership agreement spelling out the specific details of their business. This included establishing how profits would be allocated among them, what percentage of expenses would be paid by each, what resources would be required and how they would be shared, the financial structure of the business, who would have signing authority on cheques, and rules concerning any borrowing for the business. They also adopted specific protocols about taking on clients, maintaining confidentiality, avoiding conflicts, and ensuring clients they take on fit with their individual strengths.

Each paralegal would maintain his or her own professional liability insurance in compliance with By-Law 7 under the *Law Society Act*. They would also jointly maintain content insurance for the office.

The agreement states that the new firm is governed by the *Partnerships Act* and will be known as Wilson, Watson and Clarke LLP. The firm's name was registered and appears on all of its letterhead, correspondence, marketing, and documentation.

Corporation

A **corporation** is a business organization that has a legal existence separate and apart from that of the individuals who created it or who operate it.

Corporations are characterized by a specific and required division of powers. They are owned collectively by shareholders, who are entitled to a share of corporate assets. Shareholders elect directors to manage the corporation, appointing and hiring officers. Officers are the employees of a corporation; they are responsible for its operation on a day-to-day basis. The same individual(s) can act in all three capacities (shareholder, director, and officer), but the titles and roles of each position remain distinct.

The primary advantages of corporations are flexibility and limited liability. Flexibility results from the fact that the owners of the business can change without altering the business itself; contracts and staffing, among other things, remain in place through changes in ownership. Regarding limited liability, in general the owners (shareholders) of a corporation are not personally liable for the debts and liabilities of the corporation. This means that only the assets owned by the corporation may be used to satisfy its liabilities, not the owners' personal assets.

Although advantageous to entrepreneurs because of the limited liability they provide, corporations are more complex to set up and maintain than partnerships or sole proprietorships. Those who own, direct, or operate corporations must file annual reports, and shareholders must hold periodic meetings to elect directors. As a result of the different individuals and procedures involved, entrepreneurs generally have less control over a corporation than over a sole proprietorship.

> **corporation**
> a business entity that has a legal existence separate and apart from that of the individuals who created it or who operate it

Professional Corporations

Paralegals and lawyers who wish to provide legal services in Ontario and who have decided to incorporate for that purpose may only do so through a particular kind of corporation called a **professional corporation**. Sections 61.0.1(1)(b) and (c) of the *Law Society Act* specifically permit paralegals to provide legal services through professional corporations. The name of the professional corporation must include the words "Professional Corporation." A professional corporation must hold a valid **certificate of authorization** as outlined in section 61.0.7 of the *Law Society Act* and By-Law 7, part II, sections 5 and 6, and is governed by certain rules. The professional corporation must apply for, and obtain, the certificate of authorization from the LSUC (By-Law 7, part II, s 5). There are certain conditions of receiving the certificate, including a requirement that the corporation is in compliance with the *Business Corporations Act*[7] and that all individuals who will be providing legal services on behalf of the corporation are properly licensed with the LSUC.

Paralegals whose businesses do not comply with the LSUC certificate and other requirements risk losing their licences.

Most significantly, the *Business Corporations Act* imposes personal liability in certain circumstances on individuals who practise within professional corporations. Sections 3.1 to 3.4 of that Act set out a framework under which professionals are

> **professional corporation**
> a corporation that protects shareholder-owners against personal liability but not against professional liability; must be authorized by the LSUC

> **certificate of authorization**
> a certificate issued by the LSUC that permits a corporation to provide legal services

---

7 RSO 1990, c B.16.

required to perform tasks diligently and may be personally liable for failing to meet the appropriate standard. In this way, professional corporations are similar to limited liability partnerships—while professional corporations will protect the shareholder-owners against liability for general debts or liability, such as a slip and fall on the premises, they will not protect them against liability for professional negligence, such as missing a limitation period. This exception preserves accountability and protects clients.

Unlike a partnership or sole proprietorship, a corporation does not automatically come into being but must be "incorporated"—that is, created by a prescribed legal process set out in statute and in regulations. Corporations may be created under the federal corporate law statute, the *Canada Business Corporations Act*,[8] or under provincial statutes. As previously mentioned, in Ontario, the relevant statute is the *Business Corporations Act*.

The LSUC requires the corporation to be incorporated prior to the application for the certificate of authorization. A copy of the business's **articles of incorporation** must be submitted with that application. That certificate of authorization must be obtained before the legal services are provided by shareholders and/or employees of the professional corporation. In addition, shareholders in paralegals' professional corporations must be persons licensed to provide legal services in Ontario. Licensees who are applying for certificates of authorization to form professional corporations must be in good standing with the LSUC.

It is not as easy to "wind up" or terminate a professional corporation as it is to dissolve a partnership or sole proprietorship. Sections 10 and 14 of By-Law 7 require the professional corporation to apply to the LSUC for permission to surrender the certificate of authorization and to receive that permission prior to winding up that professional corporation.

> Darlene Royal and Kyle Morton are licensed paralegals who have decided to carry on business together, sharing office space, equipment, clients, and bank accounts. They have also obtained articles of incorporation and have applied for a certificate of authorization from the LSUC. If the certificate is issued, Darlene and Kyle will have formed a professional corporation.

Multi-Discipline Practices

Part III of By-Law 7 permits licensees (including partnerships and professional corporations) to form associations or partnerships with non-licensees who practise professions that support or supplement the provision of legal services—for example, accountants. These are known as **multi-discipline practices (MDPs)**. An application for approval of the MDP is submitted to the LSUC (at the time of writing, no fee) and once approved, the licensees who formed the MDP must submit a Report on Multi-Discipline Partnership by January 31 of each year. The non-licensees in the MDP must agree to be bound by the LSUC *Paralegal Rules of Conduct, Paralegal*

articles of incorporation
a document filed with the appropriate government authority that provides for incorporation as of right, provided that the required steps are followed

multi-discipline practice (MDP)
Lawyers and licensed paralegals may form a Multi-Discipline Practice with professionals who practise a profession, trade, or occupation that supports or supplements their practise of law or provision of legal service (e.g., accountants, tax consultants, trademark and patent agents, etc.)

---

8   RSC 1985, c C-44.

Professional Conduct Guidelines ("the Guidelines"),[9] and By-Laws,[10] and the *Law Society Act* and its regulations in the same way that paralegals are bound. Rule 8.01(5) specifically requires paralegals to

> ensure that non-licensee partners and associates comply with these rules and all ethical principles that govern a paralegal in the discharge of his or her professional obligations.

Finally, Rule 3.04(14) requires paralegals to ensure that the rules concerning conflicts of interest are complied with by those non-licensee partners and associates.

Associations

An association is two or more paralegals who typically share office and meeting space, reception, support staff, office equipment, and administrative facilities but who do not enter into a partnership agreement or form a professional corporation. Rule 8.02(2), which sets out restrictions concerning the provision of legal services, must be respected and the paralegal must be careful not to mislead clients into believing that the paralegals are members of the same firm. Paralegals operating in association will share costs, but do not share profits (a key factor in the determination of whether a business is a partnership rather than an association).

Operating in association with one or more paralegals offers several advantages:

- it may lead to referrals from those paralegals,
- it reduces expenses, and
- it provides access to other paralegals who may have expertise in areas in which the paralegal does not practise.

Additional LSUC Requirements

In addition to ensuring compliance with the laws and regulations that apply to all Canadian and Ontario businesses, paralegals must comply with the LSUC rules for choosing a business form and starting their businesses outlined in By-Law 7. For example, paralegals who operate limited liability partnerships must identify their partnerships as such, and each partner must carry professional liability insurance in accordance with By-Law 6, part II, section 12(1). With regard to name requirements, corporations that provide legal services are regulated, "professional" corporations whose names are governed by section 3 of By-Law 7. For example, only companies that include several licensed professionals may use the term "and associates." Paralegals may apply to the LSUC for a certificate stating that the Society does not object to a particular proposed corporate name (ss 4(1) and (2)). At the time of writing, there is no fee for this application.

---

9   Law Society of Upper Canada, *Paralegal Professional Conduct Guidelines* (1 October 2014; amendments current to 2016), online: <http://www.lsuc.on.ca/paralegal-conduct-guidelines>.

10   Law Society of Upper Canada, By-Laws, online: <https://www.lsuc.on.ca/by-laws>.

The Rules also apply to the naming of paralegal businesses. Rule 8.03(1) specifically states that the word "marketing" includes the name of the business. Rule 8.03(2) then sets out the restrictions on marketing:

> (2) A paralegal may market legal services only if the marketing
> (a) is demonstrably true, accurate and verifiable;
> (b) is neither misleading, confusing, or deceptive, nor likely to mislead, confuse or deceive; and
> (c) is in the best interests of the public and is consistent with a high standard of professionalism.

By-Law 7, part II, section 3 essentially replicates the above provision in the context of professional corporations.

In addition, the LSUC has prepared a document entitled "Paralegal Firm Name Guidelines" that it will consult as it determines whether a firm name is acceptable (see Box 3.1).

Finding Information

As a paralegal, you must be familiar with the Rules, the Guidelines, the LSUC By-Laws, and all other regulations that apply to your business. Continuing education through legal education seminars is recommended to keep your professional knowledge in these areas current. You can also find information regarding incorporation, corporate filings, tax matters, and so on online. Use only official websites, such as government websites or the LSUC's website. The LSUC's Resources for Paralegals page (<https://www.lsuc.on.ca/for-paralegals/resources-for-paralegals>) contains information on practice management topics such as business structures.

Business Name Registration

Section 2(2) of Ontario's *Business Names Act* requires the names of sole proprietorships to be registered with the Ministry of Government and Consumer Services only where these differ from the legal name of the sole proprietor.[11] For example, if your name is Frank Oz and you operate under the name "Frank Oz, Paralegal," no registration is required. However, if you wish to operate as "Frank's Legal Services," you must register this name with the Central Production and Verification Services Branch. The same is true of partnerships (ss 2(3) and (4)). There is an application form designated for sole proprietorships and partnerships (Form 1).[12]

---

11 ServiceOntario, "Registering Your Business Name" (22 August 2016), online: <https://www.ontario.ca/page/registering-your-business-name>.

12 Registration Form 1 under the Business Names Act—Sole Proprietorship/Partnership, available on the Ontario Central Forms Repository website at <http://www.forms.ssb.gov.on.ca/mbs/ssb/forms/ssbforms.nsf?opendatabase&ENV=WWE>.

Box 3.1   Paralegal Firm Name Guidelines

The following guidelines are used by staff to assist in determining whether a firm name, or a proposed firm name, complies with the *Law Society Act*, the Law Society's By-Laws, and the *Paralegal Rules of Conduct*. Each firm name, or proposed firm name, is considered on its own merits on a case-by-case basis.

1. A firm name may not include language that would imply a connection to a specific geographic location. Legal clinics under the *Legal Aid Service Act, 1998* may continue to use names that indicate a connection with the communities they serve, in keeping with the purpose of the clinic structure.

2. A firm name may not include language that would imply a connection with a government agency or with a public or charitable legal services organization (i.e. legal clinic).

3. A firm name may not include language that would imply a connection with a cultural, racial, ethnic, or religious group or organization. Legal clinics under the *Legal Aid Service Act, 1998* may continue to use names that indicate a connection with the communities they serve, in keeping with the purpose of the clinic structure.

4. A firm name may not contain language that would imply a connection with any other entity or organization not already enumerated (e.g., University Legal Services Clinic, Osgoode Hall Paralegal Office, etc.).

5. A firm name may not include language that would imply that the firm was the only or the best firm (e.g., "The" Paralegal Firm).

6. A firm name may not include language that would imply a comparison between the services performed by that firm and other firms (e.g., Best Legal Services Firm, Greatest Paralegal Firm, etc.).

7. A firm name may not contain language that would be misleading as to the number of paralegals practising with the firm, or their status in the firm.

8. A firm name may not include language that would imply the existence of a partnership, association, or affiliation between paralegals when no such relationship exists (i.e., two sole practitioners who share office space carrying on business under a common firm name).

9. A firm name may not include language that is specifically prohibited by statute (e.g., *Business Names Act*, *Business Corporations Act*, Ontario *Human Rights Code*, *Partnerships Act*, *Patent Act*, *Trade-marks Act*, *Copyright Act*).

10. A firm name may not include language that is demeaning, degrading, or derogatory.

11. A firm name should not be too general or only descriptive (e.g., Landlord and Tenant Paralegal Firm, Traffic Tickets Legal Services Firm, etc.).

12. The name of a professional corporation must include the words "Professional Corporation" or "Société professionnelle" and may not include the word "Limited," "Limitée," "Incorporated," or "Incorporée," or the corresponding abbreviations "Ltd.," "Ltée," or "Inc."

Source: Law Society of Upper Canada, "Paralegal Firm Name Guidelines," online: <http://www.lsuc.on.ca/WorkArea/DownloadAsset.aspx?id=2147491158>.

Before registering a business name (other than the name of the sole proprietor or partners in a partnership or a numbered name if a corporation), a **NUANS (Newly Upgraded Automated Name Search)** is conducted. This checks the name of the proposed business against business names that are already being used. Trademarks are also checked. This is done so that the registered name will not duplicate an existing business's name. For corporations, the NUANS must be dated within 90 days of the submission of the articles of incorporation. NUANS are obtained from private search companies such as Dye & Durham. The fee for electronic registration of a business name is lower than the fee for registering the business name in person or by mail. If you fail to register a business name (other than your own name) as a sole proprietor, you may face a fine of $2,000 (*Business Names Act*, s 10(1)).

Partnerships must register their business's name with the Ministry of Government and Consumer Services, Central Production and Verification Services Branch, where these are not simply a list of the partners' names. As mentioned above, there is an application form designated for partnerships and sole proprietorships (Form 1). Section 44.3 of the *Partnerships Act* requires limited liability partnerships to register their firm names under the *Business Names Act*. Because the names of corporations are registered at the time of incorporation, corporations are not required to do a separate name registration.

Taxes and Federal Business Registrations

When choosing a form for your business, you should consider the treatment of each form by the income tax laws of Canada. Tax issues can significantly affect the profitability of a business.

As noted, in a sole proprietorship there is no legal distinction between the owner of the business and the business itself. Therefore, on their personal income tax returns, sole proprietors include the profits or losses of their business along with their income from any other sources. Similarly, because a partnership has no separate legal existence from that of the partners, each partner reports his or her share of the partnership's profits on his or her personal income tax return. For sole proprietors acting in association with other paralegals, net professional income, which amounts to fees billed less expenses incurred to earn those fees, is included in their income for tax purposes. The individual's income tax filing deadline applies to sole proprietors. In general, the corporate tax rate is lower than that applied to individuals, which means that when a sole proprietor or partner's business is making a profit, this can be a real disadvantage. However, if the business is operating at a loss (as many businesses do during the first two to three years), this can be an advantage because the business losses can be offset against other income earned by the sole proprietor or partner, reducing the amount of income tax payable.

Incorporating a business entails tax advantages. As noted above, corporations are taxed separately from their owners, and in general the corporate tax rate is significantly lower than the individual tax rate. However, there are costs associated with obtaining this lower tax rate. The Canada Revenue Agency (CRA) can provide information and assistance regarding tax issues with respect to corporations, but it is advisable for the owners of a corporation to enlist the services of an accountant to ensure that income taxes are filed properly and that the appropriate financial records are maintained. The accountant can also assist the corporation to determine when the corporation's year-end will be for tax purposes. Finally, moneys paid to share-holders as dividends or to officers or directors in remuneration—for example, in the form of salaries or bonuses—are taxable as income to the individuals who receive them.

A paralegal business that has employees or that has provided more than $30,000 worth of legal services in a year will require a business number (BN). A BN is ob-tained from the Canada Revenue Agency. That BN is required to open a program ac-count such as a payroll account. If your business will have employees, then before you hire those employees, you will need to open a payroll account to file any source deduction remittances, such as employment insurance, income tax, and Canada Pen-sion Plan remittances on behalf of those employees. A BN is required in order to col-lect and remit GST/HST. The BN is also required to apply for an income tax number (professional corporations only). As a separate legal entity, the professional corpor-ation is taxed separately from its shareholders.

In addition, pursuant to section 125(7) of the *Income Tax Act*,[13] Canadian-con-trolled small businesses, known as "Canadian-controlled private corporations" or CCPCs, may qualify for lower tax rates. For CCPCs claiming the small business de-duction, the net tax rate is currently 10 percent. On January 1, 2018 it will decrease to 9.5 percent, and on January 1, 2019 it will decrease to 9 percent. Because Ontario has entered into an agreement with the CRA with respect to corporate tax collection, the provincial income tax rate for income eligible for the federal small business de-duction is 4.5 percent. There is generally a limit imposed on the reduced tax rate, but this can be a significant advantage. Detailed information on the tax rates can be found on the Canada Revenue Agency website. A professional corporation that qual-ifies as a CCPC may choose to pay salaries or bonuses to its shareholders to reduce the professional corporation's income in order to qualify for the lower tax rate.

Annual Filing with the LSUC

By-Law 8, part II, section 5 requires all licensed paralegals to submit an annual re-port to the LSUC each year before March 31. The report asks paralegals to provide details regarding their provision of legal services, as well as financial activities, dur-ing the relevant year. There is no fee for filing. However, failure to file in a timely manner will result in a $100 late fee and may result in the paralegal's administrative suspension by the LSUC.[14]

---

13 RSC 1985, c 1 (5th Supp).
14 See Law Society of Upper Canada, "File the Paralegal Annual Report," online: <http://www.lsuc .on.ca/For-Paralegals/About-Your-Licence/File-the-Paralegal-Annual-Report>.

Licences

In addition to the LSUC's licensing requirements for paralegals, additional business licensing requirements may apply to businesses in particular provinces or municipalities. All businesses in Ontario are subject to licensing laws, and each municipal government has the authority to issue business licences within its geographic area or jurisdiction.

If you wish to operate a business, you are responsible for determining which local by-laws, regulations, and other rules will affect your business. The best way to find out is by contacting the clerk of the municipality in which your business will operate. You can find telephone numbers on the appropriate municipal government's website or in the telephone directory's blue pages.

Licences—Sole Proprietorships and Partnerships

In Ontario, at the time of registration of the business name, sole proprietors and partnerships will be issued a Master Business Licence, which is valid for five years. The Central Production and Verification Services Branch of the Ministry of Government and Consumer Services also assigns a Business Identification Number to the business once the business name has been registered. In the event of a dissolution of the sole proprietorship or partnership, the business name registration should be cancelled. This can be done online and there is currently no fee to cancel that registration. Professional corporations do not require this because they are assigned corporation numbers upon incorporation.

Licences—Franchises

franchise
a licence granting the right to use trademarks, trade names, business methods, and systems for products and services

franchisor
the one who grants the licence

franchisee
the one to whom the licence is granted

A **franchise** is not technically a separate business structure, but a licence given by a **franchisor** to a **franchisee**. A franchise is a licence granting the franchisee the right to use trademarks, trade names, and business systems while delivering products or services—here, legal services. In return for granting this right, the franchisor (the one who grants the licence) is given the right to receive royalties from the franchisee (the one who receives the licence). There are some special considerations related to franchises, but a detailed discussion of those special considerations is beyond the scope of this textbook. Several paralegal businesses in Ontario operate as franchises.

Zoning and Building

Zoning refers to the legal use of property. Zoning laws can limit where legal services businesses may operate and set conditions for their operation. Canada Business Ontario provides useful information regarding the municipal requirements for starting a business, including the applicability of zoning laws. Prospective paralegal entrepreneurs in Ontario should consult with their local municipal governments to determine what zoning laws may apply to them. There may also be by-laws that apply to signage and parking.

In addition to zoning laws, Ontario's municipalities administer laws and regulations with regard to buildings. The *Building Code*[15] governs both the construction of new buildings and the maintenance and renovation of existing ones, including office premises.

The Home Office

The increasing use of technology in the provision of legal services has made law-related professions more portable, and home-based businesses are viable options for more legal services providers. Operating a business from home has many appealing aspects. You will save significantly on overhead costs, especially at the outset, and will not have to spend time commuting. In addition, you can claim a portion of your household expenses—such as heating and mortgage payments—against your business income for income tax purposes.

However, home offices have their disadvantages, such as encroachment on personal time and space; the fact that it may be more difficult to "leave" work may increase stress levels. There may also be safety issues with respect to clients visiting you at home. It may be possible to rent boardroom space for this purpose on an as-needed basis in a local office building, your condominium corporation, or a public library.

Before setting up a home office, you may wish to confirm that small home businesses are allowed by the zoning by-laws in your neighbourhood and, if you live in a condominium corporation, by the condominium's by-laws. You should also update your home insurance policy to ensure coverage of your business assets. Additional issues concerning maintaining client confidentiality will be discussed in Chapter 6.

Insurance

The LSUC requires paralegals who practise in Ontario to carry errors and omissions insurance, also known as professional liability insurance (By-Law 6, part II, s 12(1)). At the time of writing, paralegals must carry $1 million in liability insurance and $2 million in aggregate liability insurance (where there are multiple claims). In addition, the maximum deductible amount must be reasonable as it pertains to the financial resources of the practising paralegal. Visit the Frequently Asked Questions section of the LSUC's website for a list of providers who meet the LSUC requirements. The LSUC also requires that it be added to the policy as an additional insured and that it be given written notice a minimum of 60 days before the policy is cancelled or amended.

You will also need to insure your premises and the contents of your office, and obtain occupier's liability insurance to protect you in the event that anyone is injured while at your office. If you are renting office space, your lease agreement will set out the insurance coverage required by your landlord. Your insurer will likely ask for a copy of your lease in order to ensure that you are purchasing appropriate coverage.

---

15 O Reg 332/12.

You may wish to consider purchasing business interruption insurance, which will provide you with compensation in the event that you are unable to operate for a period of time as a result of a fire or other calamity. Finally, as a self-employed person, you should consider purchasing health and dental, life, and—most importantly—disability insurance, for both yourself and any employees.

Conclusion

Paralegals in Ontario may conduct their business in the form of a sole proprietorship, as either general partnerships or limited liability partnerships, or in the form of a professional corporation. Each business form carries advantages and disadvantages, and each is governed by different legislation, including federal and provincial laws and regulations. By-Law 7 outlines LSUC requirements for different business entities.

Although relatively simple to set up and wind down, sole proprietorships have, among other disadvantages, unlimited personal liability, meaning that sole proprietors can lose personal assets if unable to pay their business debts.

In partnerships, two or more persons carry on business together with a reasonable expectation of making a profit. Sharing marketing, premises, and staff allows them to conduct their business with greater efficiency. Like sole proprietors, partners bear personal liability for all obligations entered into on behalf of the partnership. They may be held jointly and severally liable in any court judgments, including claims of professional negligence.

Limited liability partnerships offer limited liability with respect to the professional negligence of partners, meaning that if one partner is successfully sued, the other partners are not jointly and severally liable for the amount of the judgment.

Paralegals may also provide legal services in association with other paralegals, sharing the costs of leasing office space, renting or buying office equipment and supplies, and employing support staff. In an association those paralegals do not share profits earned by the business. Paralegals may also join other professionals to form multi-discipline practices.

Paralegals and lawyers who wish to operate professional corporations must obtain a valid certificate of authorization from the LSUC. The *Law Society Act* imposes personal liability in certain circumstances on individuals who practise within professional corporations—they must perform tasks diligently and may be personally liable for failing to meet the appropriate standard.

Operating your business from home will save you money and time in overhead costs and commuting, but a home office may encroach on your personal time and space, and raise safety concerns with respect to client visits. Regardless of the type of business you operate or where you operate from, you will require errors and omissions insurance and should consider what additional types of insurance—such as occupier's liability, life, health and dental, and disability insurance—you may require or may wish to obtain.

KEY TERMS

articles of incorporation, 28
bankruptcy, 22
certificate of authorization, 27
corporation, 27
fiduciary duty, 25
franchise, 34
franchisee, 34
franchisor, 34
insolvency, 22
joint and several liability, 24
limited liability partnership, 25
limited partnership, 25
multi-discipline practice (MDP), 28
NUANS (Newly Upgraded Automated Name Search), 32
partnership, 24
professional corporation, 27

USEFUL URLS

Building Code, O Reg 332/12. <http://canlii.ca/t/52vfv>.

Business Corporations Act, RSO 1990, c B.16. <http://canlii.ca/t/52vtz>.

Canada Business Corporations Act, RSC 1985, c C-44. <http://canlii.ca/t/52f1j>.

Canada Business Ontario. "Closing or Selling Your Business." <http://www.cbo-eco.ca/en/index.cfm/managing/exiting-your-business/closing-or-selling-your-business>.

Canada Revenue Agency. "Corporation Tax Rates." <http://www.cra-arc.gc.ca/tx/bsnss/tpcs/crprtns/rts-eng.html>.

Canada Revenue Agency. "Do You Need a Business Number or a Program Account?" <http://www.cra-arc.gc.ca/tx/bsnss/tpcs/bn-ne/wrks-eng.html>.

Canada Revenue Agency. "Sole Proprietorships and Partnerships." <http://www.cra-arc.gc.ca/tx/bsnss/tpcs/slprtnr/menu-eng.html>.

Law Society of Upper Canada. "Guide to Opening Your Practice for Paralegals." <http://www.lsuc.on.ca/with.aspx?id=2147499334>.

Law Society of Upper Canada. "Home Office." <http://www.lsuc.on.ca/HomeOffice>.

Law Society of Upper Canada. "Paralegal Firm Name Guidelines." Link to this document from the "Guide to Opening Your Practice for Paralegals." <http://www.lsuc.on.ca/with.aspx?id=2147499334>.

Law Society of Upper Canada. *Paralegal Rules of Conduct* (2007, as amended). <http://www.lsuc.on.ca/paralegal-conduct-rules>.

Law Society of Upper Canada. *Paralegal Professional Conduct Guidelines* (2008). <http://www.lsuc.on.ca/paralegal-conduct-guidelines>.

Ministry of Municipal Affairs and Ministry of Housing. "Ontario Building Code." <http://www.mah.gov.on.ca/Page7393.aspx>.

REVIEW QUESTIONS

1. What is a sole proprietorship?

2. What is a partnership?

3. What is a professional corporation?

4. What is a franchise? Can you identify three Ontario paralegal firms that are franchised?

5. What is the difference between a partnership and an association?

6. What is the chief advantage of a limited liability partnership?

7. What is an advantage available to small businesses that are Canadian-controlled private corporations?

8. In a limited liability partnership, are partners responsible for contractual debts incurred by the partnership?

9. What is the amount of professional liability insurance that practising paralegals in Ontario are currently required to carry?

10. If a partnership's name consists only of the names of the partners, must it register the firm name pursuant to the *Business Names Act*?

SCENARIO-BASED QUESTIONS

1. Name That Business

Samantha Brooks has decided to open a paralegal firm and to organize it as a sole proprietorship. For the first two years she is going to work alone. She is trying to come up with a name for the business. These are her top five choices:

1. Ottawa Legal Services
2. Top Ranked Legal Services
3. Samantha Brooks and Associates
4. Samantha Brooks LLP
5. Small Claims Paralegals

Consult the Paralegal Firm Name Guidelines to determine which, if any, of these names is likely to be acceptable to the LSUC.

2. Bringing in the Business

Maxwell Lake is a newly licensed paralegal. He has hired a receptionist for his brand new office but has no other employees. Maxwell thinks he will get more business if he puts "Maxwell Lake & Associates" on his letterhead. Should Maxwell do this? Why or why not?

3. Partner Problem

Monique Lachance is a licensed paralegal. For the first two years after opening her practice Monique ran it out of her home. Monique's cousin, Pierre Moran, has just obtained his paralegal licence. Before he was licensed, Pierre did his placement hours under Monique's supervision. Monique has decided that it is time to expand her business and that she will do this by giving Pierre a job. She feels that he needs further training before he accepts clients of his own and initially plans to employ him as a receptionist and file clerk, and to gradually give him more responsibility. If Pierre proves himself to her, she will entrust him with his own clients. Does this mean that Pierre is Monique's partner? Why or why not? Does your answer change if, 18 months later, Pierre is entrusted with his own clients? Why or why not?

4. Identification Please

John Jones and Lucy Lee are licensed paralegals. They share an office, receptionist, telephone number, photocopier, and all office equipment. Retainers received from new and existing clients are paid into one trust account. John and Lucy use letterhead and business cards that say "Jones and Lee licensed paralegals." What type of business entity is "Jones and Lee"? Why did you reach that conclusion?

5. Expense Arrangements

Priyah Kaur and Leon Noble are licensed paralegals. Priyah has been licensed for five years while Leon has been licensed for three years. Priyah's practice deals mainly with administrative law while Leon's largely deals with provincial offences matters. For three years their offices were across the hall from each other in a busy office building. Priyah, whose practice is very busy, sometimes refers clients to Leon when her clients consult her about matters outside her area of expertise. Leon and Priyah have become friendly and recently decided that they can save a great deal of money by leasing one suite in their building. They will be sharing meeting rooms and a receptionist, and they have agreed that Priyah will pay for 60 percent of the office equipment expenses from her business's general account while Leon will pay for 40 percent of those expenses. What type of arrangement is this? Explain your conclusion.

Planning for Start-Up

4

LEARNING OUTCOMES

After completing this chapter, you should be able to:

- Create a business plan.

- Understand the purpose of client and market profiles and how to develop them.

- Understand the purpose of market analysis and a marketing plan.

- Understand basic principles of sound financial planning and analysis, including start-up costs and cash flow analysis.

- Create a management plan.

- Strategize for effective implementation of plans.

Business Plan

A **business plan** is a document that contains a summary of a business's operational and financial objectives, along with detailed plans and budgets that explain how the objectives will be achieved. A business plan is for a paralegal business as crucial and foundational as architectural plans are for a building; few people would ride an elevator to the top of the CN Tower if the building was not professionally designed and expertly engineered. Legal services entrepreneurs should consider consulting professionals and should look carefully at available sources of start-up funding when developing their business plans. A detailed and realistic business plan makes planning a business more manageable and more effective.

Business plans evolve as new information is gathered and as circumstances change, so it is important to be flexible, but having a detailed framework prior to start-up is equally important. A business plan can test the practicality of a business idea; it is a risk-free rehearsal for opening the business. Because they allow flaws to be identified and corrected (or at least minimized) before implementation, business plans can provide huge savings in time and money. The alternative process of trial and error can be extremely costly.

A detailed business plan is also often necessary for acquiring capital from third parties. Banks more readily grant loans to, and investors are more willing to become involved in, a business that has detailed plans available for their review and assessment.

The components of business plans vary, but generally include

- client and market profiles;
- market analysis;
- the business's mission and/or vision;
- a marketing plan;
- an operating plan (detailing location, facilities, equipment, and staff);
- a financial plan;
- appendixes (incorporation documents, resumés of key management players, leases for office space and equipment, the licences of paralegals providing legal services, shareholder or partnership agreements, copies of academic credentials, and so on);
- milestones (objectives, goals, and action plans with dates); and
- **SWOT analysis** of competitors.

Your business plan should be specific and detailed enough to allow you to make financially sound decisions and take reasonable risks.

Client and Market Profiles

An important way to assess opportunities for your business's future success is by creating client and market profiles. A **client profile** is data relating to the demographics of your potential clients, such as

- geographic location,
- age,
- income level,
- gender,
- ethnicity, and
- education level.

The client profile will allow you to assess the needs of your target market. It can help you understand who your clients will likely be, how to find them, and how to motivate them to purchase your services. For example, if your clients are renters, they may need representation with respect to landlord and tenant matters; if they are immigrants, they may need immigration advice.

Client profile information can be culled from a variety of sources, including Statistics Canada, the Canada Mortgage and Housing Corporation (CMHC), and Ontario's Ministry of Economic Development, Employment and Infrastructure.

> Lucas Evans has decided to open a home-based paralegal firm in Mississauga, Ontario. His research has revealed that the average income per person in Mississauga was $41,314 in 2010; there were 79,174 apartments; and the population in the 20-44 age group was 37.1 percent, with a higher percentage of females than males in that age group. He has also learned that in 2011, 89.5 percent of people in Mississauga spoke only English. Since census information on demographics is outdated, Evans has chosen to supplement his research by using the site <www.realtor.ca>, where he has narrowed down his search to the particular part of Mississauga in which he intends to locate his business. He has found that once he has pulled up a listing in the area, he can obtain information on demographics. The information provided includes population by age group, average household size, median age, average household income, languages spoken, level of education, home ownership, and occupations of residents of the area. In addition, the site makes projections about population growth going forward to 2024. Evans also intends to use the site to find commercial premises once he has secured funding for his business and is ready to move the business from his home to larger premises. See Appendix 4.1, later in this chapter, for Evans's sample business plan.

A **market profile** can provide you with important information about areas of opportunity in the market. For example, what types of legal problems are common? Which areas are underserved poorly by lawyers (for example, due to the high price of services)? Are these areas within the scope of permitted practice for paralegals? This information may help you design your website, choose the most effective

client profile
data relating to the demographics of a business's potential clients—such as their geographic location, age, income level, gender, ethnicity, and education level—that allows business owners to assess the needs of their target market

market profile
a business tool, created through research, that provides business owners with important information about areas of opportunity in the market—for example, common legal problems in a particular market

advertising media, fine-tune your marketing strategies, and determine prices for your services. The Rules and the Guidelines concerning marketing of a paralegal practice will be discussed in Chapter 5. In early 2017, the LSUC released a committee report concerning advertising by paralegals and lawyers that resulted in changes to the Rules. A business plan must be fluid enough to accommodate changes of this nature. The following scenario emphasizes the importance of adapting business plans to seize advantageous opportunities.

PLANNING FOR PRACTICE

The Perfect Plan?

In 2014, Donna Reigher decided to leave the law firm with which she was working and start her own paralegal practice focusing on small claims litigation. She intended to use her strong negotiation and mediation skills to help clients settle disputes in the settlement conference stage, saving them time and money.

Before launching her practice, she devoted significant time and effort into building her three-year business plan. She carefully considered the set-up and structure of her business. She set reasonable and realistic revenue targets and honestly assessed the workload required to meet those targets. She developed a sound and comprehensive marketing strategy that she was confident would make her business a success.

Although she had only been thinking about starting her own practice for about a year, the exercise of preparing the business plan allowed her to consider all aspects of what her business would be and the steps, funds, and resources needed to meet the goals she set.

Just a year after she started the practice, the town's largest employer—a car-part manufacturing plant—announced it would be cutting costs due to declining sales. More than 100 workers were told they would be losing their jobs within a few short months. Before launching her practice, she had worked in a law firm that counted employment law cases among its specialties and she had gained valuable experience in that area.

Sensing an opportunity to generate some extra income for her practice during its early stages, she reached out to an acquaintance who was a shop steward for the union at the plant. She had hoped he could help refer her to some of the affected workers who needed legal support after they had been notified of their severance agreements and the terms of call back. Within a week, she had more than a dozen calls from workers at the plant inquiring about their legal rights. Eight of those workers became clients.

On behalf of those clients, she was able to negotiate settlements more favourable than legally required to be provided by the employer and get the company to accept a longer period under which benefits would be paid out during the transition.

Her success with the plant workers led to more referrals and contacts from other employees in the area who were also impacted by a downturn in the local economy. That downturn created the opportunity to take her practice in a new direction.

Donna revised her business plan to reflect her new focus on employee rights in employment law. She reviewed every aspect of the plan. Based on her experience with the plant, she adjusted her fee structure and set new reasonable and attainable revenue goals. She developed a new marketing plan that included writing a weekly blog on employee rights that enhanced her standing as an expert in the field.

By seizing on opportunities that arose from changes in her own community and being willing to adapt and change to meet those opportunities, Donna was able to build a successful and growing practice and bolster her reputation as an expert in the field of employment law. Because of this, she will be ready the next time circumstances create new opportunities.

Ask yourself when you're building your business plan: Would you be willing and able to change and adapt your plan if circumstances—good or bad—occur or would you prefer to stick to the plan and make it work?

Client and market profiles are created through research. Telephone or online surveys can be useful research methods in the case of ongoing businesses, and employees may be able to compile the relevant data themselves. Once the likely target group of clients is defined, that information can be cross-referenced with information known about that particular demographic subgroup. For example, if you are providing primarily traffic law advice and your typical clients are middle-class males who have a college education and are located in a particular neighbourhood, you will want to consider what kind of advertising will appeal to them, such as ads in the autotrader, newspaper, online advertising (for example, ads that come up when people play games on their phones or tablets, or when they visit websites while using their PCs—online banner ads), online professional social network sites, or media relating to sports in the area (for example, a print ad on the boards of a hockey arena).

Market Analysis

Market analysis is used by business owners in the planning stages of their business and on an ongoing basis. It can help owners determine the opportunities and risks of a particular market and how these may affect their success. A typical market analysis considers the following factors:

market analysis
used by business owners, in the planning stages of their business and on an ongoing basis, to help them determine the opportunities and risks of a particular market and how these may affect their success

- Market growth rate: The market growth rate for future years can be extrapolated from an analysis of the growth rate in the market in the past year; although not definitive, information about the past is useful for making projections.

- Market size: The size of your market can be estimated based on information obtained from Statistics Canada, your local chamber of commerce, or neighbourhood business associations. Your own surveys may also be helpful.

- Market profitability: Can your target market afford legal services? How many will qualify for legal aid? Income information may be available from Statistics Canada. You can consult realtor.ca, but before deciding where to locate your business, it is a good idea to visit neighbourhoods in person to assess socioeconomic levels.

- Market trends: Be aware of changes to the law or demographics that may affect your business or present new opportunities. Examples are the Family Legal Services Review, which is currently underway to determine whether paralegals' scope of practice may be extended to some aspects of family law; the particular legal services needs of an aging population; and language barriers of a new group of immigrants. Keep up to date with trends by monitoring local and legal news, subscribing to news feeds, and networking with other paralegals in person and via online professional networking sites.

Marketing Plan

marketing plan
a document that sets out actions identified as necessary for a business to achieve its marketing objectives

A **marketing plan** is a document that sets out actions that are necessary for a business to achieve the marketing objectives identified through its client and market profiling. The plan should move from general to specific points, first outlining the overall objectives or "mission" of the organization, then setting out specific objectives and action plans. For example, your mission may be to become the most respected legal services provider for a particular neighbourhood, achieving both affordability and quality. Your specific objectives may be to serve new immigrants and low-income members of the community. Action plans may involve advertising in different ethnic newspapers, hiring bilingual staff and promoting this to the public, and offering free legal information at community centres and newcomers' organizations.

A marketing plan should identify what client groups are to be served (usually through client profiling), what client needs are to be met, and how those needs are to be met. A marketing plan for a small legal services business might include the following:

- a description of the specific legal services that will be provided and any aspects of the business that may set it apart, such as unique credentials, languages spoken by the members of the firm, or past experience of any of the paralegals (for example, former police officers);
- a marketing budget estimate, including a plan for advertising and promotion;
- a description of where the business will be located, and the advantages and disadvantages of that location;
- a strategy for setting fees (for example, billable hours or flat rates for services); and
- client and market profiles.

Marketing plans should be written out, since written documents serve as clear reference points that can be evaluated. Because the market will change and each action may affect other actions, the plans should be treated as works-in-progress and should be revised continuously—for example, if the demographics in your area change or if new advertising opportunities arise.

Budgeting and Financial Planning

When starting a business, making financial plans and setting budgets is critical to success. **Financial plans** are a key component of business plans. They provide a framework for measuring money coming into and going out of the business—more specifically, they show how much money is required to operate the business and where that money is coming from.

In its most basic form, a **budget** is a list of anticipated or intended income and expenses for a defined future period. Budgets facilitate realistic and accurate financial planning, allowing businesses to set goals for the future and to track and assess achievement of these goals. They can allow for control of growth, some measure of evaluation, and general planning; facilitate communication between individuals within an organization; and motivate individuals to work harder.

Budgets are typically made for periods of one year; the one-year period over which a budget runs is the *fiscal* year and does not necessarily coincide with the calendar year. Monthly budget targets may also be set. It is generally a good idea to set annual targets and then break them down by month. In the process of setting your budget, it may be useful to consult an accountant or bookkeeper; otherwise you will need to acquire basic accounting skills yourself.

Among other things, budgets predict and record **cash flow**, or the movement of money into and out of a business. To analyze cash flow is to study the cycles through which cash flows in and out. A business's accounts receivable, accounts payable, and credit all affect cash flow analysis.

Many paralegal businesses struggle with cash flow, and it is important to develop systems to ensure that clients pay for the services they receive. Collecting up-front retainers, billing regularly over the course of a file, and accepting payment by credit card are some measures that paralegal businesses can implement to protect against potential cash flow shortages.

Budgeted income for a particular period—namely, client fees paid—must be balanced against the expenditures to be made during the same time period. Expenses may include office rent, telephone, Internet, supplies, insurance, and employee salaries (including your own). In addition to these ongoing expenses, small businesses will likely incur significant one-time start-up costs—for example, purchasing computers and office furniture and paying first and last month's rent. The difference between the income and expenditures is the *profit* or *loss* for the period.

In general, it is wisest to calculate budgets on a cash basis, where only money actually spent or received during the period is included. Particularly where fees are charged for services (for example, in the work of paralegals), businesses must ensure that their budgets distinguish between money still owed to them for fees ("billable" or "billed" fees) and money they have actually received.

Budgets should be set as projections prior to the beginning of a particular period. Once the period ends, actual revenues and expenses should be tracked and compared with the expected or projected numbers. Comparing their budgeted numbers to actual ones can help businesses with their ongoing planning. They can look for

financial plan
a key component of a business plan that concerns the money coming into and going out of the business; shows how much money is required to operate the business and where that money is coming from

budget
a list of anticipated income and expenses for a defined future period

cash flow
movement of money into and out of a business

explanations for differences between anticipated and actual earnings and expenses, and through this type of **financial analysis** can determine whether they are setting appropriate fees, renting suitable office space, need to add or reduce resources or employees, and so on.

Management Plan

The **management plan** is the part of a business plan that outlines how the business is structured and describes the responsibilities of various individuals with respect to its management. The plan should set out not only who does what, but why—that is, it should outline how the particular skills and expertise of key individuals will contribute to the business's profitability. For paralegals working together, it is important to assess and understand how the work of each can complement that of the others.

If the business is a sole proprietorship, the management plan will be simple; the sole proprietor will be the decision-maker. However, if the business structure is more complex—as in a partnership or a professional corporation with more than one shareholder—the management plan becomes more critical. In these cases, the plan may include a detailed partnership agreement that sets out the responsibilities and decision-making authority of each partner, or articles of incorporation that name the directors, officers, and shareholders, and outline the responsibilities and decision-making authority of these individuals.

Basic tasks involved in most small businesses include marketing, sales, administration, and business development. Most small businesses will not have a separate individual responsible for each task. The management plan should acknowledge this and should set out the tasks that each individual has been assigned to perform, even where responsibility for a task is shared. The manner in which each member of the management team will be compensated should also be described.

Strategizing to Implement Plans

Once a business has made its plans, it must implement them effectively. In order for plans to become reality, they must be structured in such a way that they can be continuously reviewed and revised. Your business plan should include a statement of goals, objectives, tasks, and action plans. Your plan should also set dates at which the implementation of each of these will be assessed and reassessed.

The management team and the employees need to know what their specific targets are and when these should be met. When these are not met, the reasons why should be investigated. Businesses often devote significant attention to drafting their business plans but fail to pay enough attention to assessing and evaluating to what extent these are being implemented once the business is underway. Reviewing performance and measuring results are important aspects of maintaining a business.

Conclusion

Having a detailed framework prior to the start-up of your business in the form of a business plan is important to your business's eventual success. Business plans typically include client and market profiles; market analysis; a statement of the business's mission; vision; marketing, operating, and financial plans; SWOT analysis of competitors; appendixes containing a variety of additional information; and clearly outlined milestones that include objectives, goals, and action plans with dates.

Creating client and market profiles through research will allow you to assess opportunities for the future success of your business. Client profiles allow you to assess the needs of your target market through data relating to the demographics of your potential clients, while market profiles provide important information about areas of opportunity in the market.

Conducting a market analysis is another important aspect of the planning process. Typically, this involves a consideration of the market growth rate, market size, market profitability, and market trends. The information gained from market analysis will help you determine the opportunities and risks of a particular market and how these may affect their success, in the planning stages of your business and on an ongoing basis.

Marketing plans set out actions that are necessary for a business to achieve the marketing objectives identified through its client and market profiling. The plans should be written out explicitly. For a small legal services business, plans should include a description of the specific legal services to be provided; a marketing budget estimate, including a plan for advertising and promotion; a description of where the business will be located, and the advantages and disadvantages of that location; a strategy for setting fees; and client and market profiles.

Budgets are another important planning tool, allowing businesses to set goals for the future and to track and assess achievement of those goals. When setting a budget for your business, you might consider consulting an accountant or a bookkeeper.

The tasks for which each individual who holds a management position within the organization is responsible should be set out in a management plan. In partnerships and professional corporations, the plan may include a detailed partnership agreement or articles of incorporation. Management plans should also describe the manner in which each member of the management team will be compensated.

Paralegal entrepreneurs must ensure that their plans are implemented effectively once they have been made. This involves setting dates for the assessment and reassessment of whether and how the goals, objectives, tasks, and action plans included in the business plan are being implemented and achieved.

APPENDIX 4.1

Sample Business Plan: Evans Legal Services

Note: A title page and table of contents should be included in a business plan once it has been finalized.

EVANS LEGAL SERVICES—BUSINESS PLAN

1. EXECUTIVE SUMMARY

Evans Legal Services is a new firm specializing in providing affordable legal services and legal consulting specifically to small business clients. The aim is not only to represent these businesses on legal matters, but also to counsel them on proper compliance with the multitude of laws that affect them. The business is built upon the education and experience of Lucas Evans, a candidate for paralegal licensing in 2017. Evans was a journalist for more than 15 years. He has owned and operated two small businesses and has spent the last three years working on legal issues for three associated small corporations.

Evans Legal Services will specialize in the areas of employment standards, workplace safety, civil litigation, defence of human rights claims, incorporation and legal structure, tax credits and compliance, community standards, and contracts.

The keys to success for Evans Legal Services are reputation and networking, responsiveness and quality, and generating repeat and referral clients.

Hourly legal services will be the initial primary service offered by Evans Legal Services, though contingency contracts and projects will be considered in the future.

There is an existing local market for this business that research has shown can support new and expanding legal services firms.

The paralegal profession is a growing one in Ontario, particularly since the Law Society of Upper Canada began regulating and licensing these professionals in 2007. Most paralegals work in small claims court and provincial offences court, and many of those are working for consumers against businesses. Few practising paralegals in Ontario currently report working in areas that are often highly relevant to business—namely employment standards, human rights, and Workplace Safety and Insurance Board. All fall within the paralegal scope of practice.

A vast majority of businesses in Ontario are small enterprises ranging from 1 to 100 employees in fields such as automotive, home services, retail, and technology. These are the businesses Evans Legal Services will be targeting specifically.

Evans Legal Services' success will rely heavily on "network" marketing, taking advantage of the numerous trade shows, symposiums, and directories available to small businesses in Toronto and the GTA. Marketing will also be conducted online via professional social networking sites and online classified sites, which are increasingly used by small businesses to save costs. In addition, Evans Legal Services will continue to "look out" for clients by providing periodic e-newsletters and compiling a database of emails that allow regular contact with current, potential, and former clients.

Evans Legal Services will be a sole proprietorship that will be based at home for the first year, utilizing available free and adequate meeting space available in downtown Toronto and downtown Mississauga. In the second year, Evans Legal Services will secure inexpensive office space. It has already secured most technical equipment and office furniture. Only the investment of legal accounting and research software will be significant costs to set up the practice. Start-up fees, overall, will be minimal.

Financial projections for the first two years are geared toward a modest profit of $7,209 in the first year and $9,209 in the second year. Revenue is based on three components—legal services (billable work per hour), agent fees (acting on behalf of other legal professionals), and business consulting work (tax preparation, legal compliance, etc.). It is estimated that of the roughly 160 hours of general work time per month, 88 would be spent on billable work and 72 would be spent on networking and marketing.

1.1 KEYS TO SUCCESS

The keys to success for Evans Legal Services are

- Marketing and Networking (getting the name out there)
- Responsiveness (being a reliable and responsive resource for clients)
- Quality (serving clients with professional work of the highest quality and integrity)
- Relationships (developing loyal repeat and referral clients)

Evans Legal Services will be a start-up venture with the following characteristics:

2. FIRM PROFILE

2.1 CLARITY OF OFFERING

Evans Legal Services is a legal- and business-consulting firm that aims to provide affordable legal services to small business clients and prepare clients to properly comply with a multitude of laws that affect their enterprises.

2.2 BACKGROUND

Evans Legal Services is built on the education and experience of Lucas Evans, a highly accomplished journalist with more than 15 years' experience in that business. He was the principal of his own media relations firm from 2003-2008 and was the creator and publisher of his own lifestyles magazine for five years from 2009-2014. During this time, he has built a solid background in business law, and effective March 2017, he will be licensed as a paralegal by the Law Society of Upper Canada.

While attending college for paralegal studies in Ontario, Evans has also worked full-time for three small businesses based in Mississauga, Ontario—an automobile supply company, a holding company, and a property management and acquisition company. He has been active in dealing with a multitude of legal issues for these companies, including landlord-and-tenant issues and employment standards matters.

Evans is a candidate for paralegal licensing with the Law Society of Upper Canada in 2017.

2.3 LEGAL STATUS OF BUSINESS

Evans Legal Services will operate as a sole proprietorship for the first two years. The name will be registered with the Province of Ontario prior to the planned start of business January 1, 2018. The plan beyond the first two years is to fully register as a professional corporation.

2.4 MISSION STATEMENT

Evans Legal Services provides outstanding legal representation to small businesses and ongoing knowledge to help those businesses function within ever-changing legal frameworks.

2.5 VISION STATEMENT

Evans Legal Services will be a highly reputable legal- and business-consulting firm fully specializing in small business operations.

2.6 AIMS AND OBJECTIVES

Evans Legal Services aims to be a widely respected small business legal firm. Evans Legal Services will strive to provide outstanding legal representation to all clients and provide ongoing preparation and advice that helps small businesses thrive in an often-complicated legal environment of which many small entrepreneurs are not fully aware.

2.7 SERVICES PROVIDED

Evans Legal Services will be providing the following services in accordance with the Law Society of Upper Canada's paralegal scope of practice. Tax work is not part of the provision of legal services.

- Civil litigation
- Workplace Safety and Insurance Board claims
- Employment standards claims and charges
- Human rights claims

2.8 STAFFING REQUIREMENTS

For the first year of operations, Evans Legal Services will essentially be a one-person home-based operation, relying heavily on Evans's past experience in accounting and practice management to meet the obligations of this business. During the second year, he anticipates renting office space in an executive suite set-up that will include receptionist services, and perhaps hiring an accountant or assistant, though plans do not currently allow for that.

2.9 FUTURE PLANS

Once Evans Legal Services is fully established, plans are to expand the operation to include additional legal professionals (paralegals) and small business professionals from other disciplines, including accounting and tax specialists, in a more full-service and dynamic firm.

3. MARKET RESEARCH

3.1 INFORMATION ON LEGAL SERVICES PROVIDERS

According to the Canadian Association of Paralegals, the paralegal profession is one of the fastest growing professions today. A large contributor to that growth was the introduction of licensing for paralegals in Ontario in 2007. That licensing brought paralegals under the regulatory umbrella of the Law Society of Upper Canada.

Licensed paralegals in Ontario are permitted to provide legal services within a specific scope of practice. That scope includes representing clients in the following areas:

- civil matters worth less than $25,000 in Small Claims Court;
- provincial offences in the Ontario Court of Justice under the quasi-criminal *Provincial Offences Act*;
- matters at quasi-judicial boards, agencies, commissions, and tribunals, such as the Landlord and Tenant Board, Human Rights Tribunal of Ontario, and the Ontario Labour Relations Board; and
- summary conviction criminal matters with a maximum penalty of six months in jail and/or a $5,000 fine.

Of course, legal fees vary from one practising paralegal to the next, but in broad terms fees are between 30 and 50 percent that of lawyers. Because the paralegal scope of practice generally serves clients who might otherwise have difficulty or be unable to afford the higher rates of lawyers, the public has greater access to legal services that are more affordable under the regulatory scheme. Therefore, paralegals are increasingly in demand.

According to the *Report of Appointee's Five-Year Review of Paralegal Regulation in Ontario* prepared for the Attorney General of Ontario by David Morris in 2012, there were 4,301 active paralegal licensees in Ontario and another 596 who were inactive or left the practice. A growing number of those active licensees since January 2011 have come from the growing pool of graduates from accredited paralegal programs in the province. Others come from those who were "grandfathered" in, having practised as paralegals prior to the Law Society of Upper Canada regulation of that profession.

The report further notes that 40 percent of paralegals who responded to a survey commissioned by the Law Society of Upper Canada are practising privately as sole practitioners; 26 percent are employed in a private legal/paralegal practice; and another 20 percent are listed as "otherwise employed."

The survey also found that 43 percent of respondents were most active in Small Claims Court practice, while 37 percent were active in *Provincial Offences Act* practice; 27 percent were active in Landlord and Tenant practice; and 13 percent were active in summary conviction criminal practice. Agencies and tribunal practice ranges from 8 to 18 percent of respondents.

3.2 CLIENT PROFILE

Evans Legal Services will primarily be targeting small businesses with between 5 and 100 employees in Toronto and the GTA. These clients will be in the industries of light manufacturing, financial services, marketing and communications, and wholesale distribution, among others.

According to Statistics Canada, more than 97 percent of businesses in Ontario have fewer than 100 employees (55 percent of which are micro-enterprises of 1-4 employees). Of the 1,138,761 employer businesses, 2,708 (about 0.2 percent) have 500 employees or more, 1,116,423 (98 percent) have fewer than 100 employees, 75 percent have fewer than 10 employees, and 55 percent have only 1 to 4 employees.

About one quarter of all business locations produce goods, whereas the remainder provide services. Small firms (those with fewer than 100 employees) make up 98 percent of goods-producing employer businesses and 98 percent of all service-producing employer businesses. Using an alternative definition of small businesses in the service-producing sector—small businesses as those with fewer than 50 employees—it can be said that small firms account for 96 percent of all service-producing employer firms.

The distribution of employer businesses by size of business location in each industry shows the greatest variation among micro-enterprises. The highest percentages of micro-industries are in professional, scientific, and technical services (74.8 percent) and in agriculture, forestry, fishing, and hunting (71.4 percent). The lowest percentages of micro-enterprises are found in public administration (22.1 percent), accommodation and food services (27.9 percent), and utilities (34.1 percent).

In the GTA, key small businesses break down as follows:

Area	Number of Businesses in GTA
Arts and Culture	971
Automotive*	4,758
Food and Beverage	9,774
Health and Beauty	5,469
Home and Garden*	3,452
Computers and Technology Services	2,661
Home Services*	1,921
Fashion	3,127
Moving and Storage*	589

* Indicates area Evans Legal Services will particularly focus on.

3.3 COMPETITORS

The following are paralegals working in the target market area who market and provide services to small businesses:

Direct Competitors—Paralegal

Callahan Paralegal (Morris Callahan, licensee—Mississauga)

Unique Legal Services (Kiran Kaur, licensee—Mississauga)

Direct Competitors—Lawyer

Anderson, Carlyle (Mississauga, Toronto)

Midas, Gold, and Brown, LLP (Toronto)

Silver and Harris, LLP (Mississauga)

3.4 COMPETITOR SWOT ANALYSIS

	Strengths	Weaknesses	Opportunity	Threats
Callahan Paralegal (Morris Callahan)	Ten years in the business, specializing in small claims cases. Licensed since 2008.	Practice spread out to include summary conviction criminal and tribunal work. Many clients are individuals suing businesses.	Specialize in representing small businesses in small claims court as well as tribunals.	Strong professional networks.
Unique Legal Services (Kiran Kaur)	15+ years of legal experience; licensed since 2008. Experience in small claims.	Primary focus of her business appears to be working as an agent for lawyers.	Specialize in representing small businesses in small claims court as well as tribunals.	Established clientele, but actively seeking to expand client base. Competitive fees for agency work.

KEY TERMS

budget, 45
business plan, 40
cash flow, 45
client profile, 41
financial analysis, 46
financial plan, 45
management plan, 46
market analysis, 43
market profile, 41
marketing plan, 44
SWOT analysis, 40

USEFUL URLS

The Balance. "Business Plans." <https://www.thebalance
.com/small-business-plans-4073881>.

Business Owners' Idea Cafe Inc. "Idea Cafe's Financing
Your Biz: Idea Cafe's Exclusive Instant All-in-One First
Year Budget Worksheet." <http://www
.businessownersideacafe.com/financing/
budget_calculator.html>.

Canada Mortgage and Housing Corporation. 2015.
"Canada's Purpose-Built Rental Vacancy Rate
Increases." <https://www.cmhc-schl.gc.ca/en/
hoficlincl/observer/observer_028.cfm?obssource
=observer-en&obsmedium=link&obscampaign
=obs-20151223-p-b-rental-vacancy-inc>.

Canadian Real Estate Association. 2016. <https://www
.realtor.ca>.

Lawpro. 2017. "Managing the Finances of Your Practice."
<http://www.practicepro.ca/Practice/
PracticeFinances.asp>.

Lawpro. 2017. "Precedent Documents and Retainers."
<http://www.practicepro.ca/practice/
financesbookletprecedents.asp> (sample business
plan, retainer agreements, etc.).

Ministry of Economic Development, Employment and
Infrastructure. 2016. <https://www.ontario.ca/page/
small-business-advice-support-services-regulations>.

NetMBA. "Market Analysis." <http://www.netmba.com/
marketing/market/analysis/>.

REVIEW QUESTIONS

1. What is a marketing plan?
2. What should a marketing plan for a small paralegal business include?
3. What is cash flow?
4. What is the purpose of budgeting?
5. What is a management plan?
6. What is a SWOT analysis?
7. What is a vision statement?

Maintaining Your Business

5

LEARNING OUTCOMES

After completing this chapter, you should be able to:

- Describe basic strategies for business communications, and explain how advertising and marketing are circumscribed by consumer protection laws as well as by Rule 8.

- Understand how to charge fees in compliance with Rule 5 and Guideline 19.

- Be aware of the various employment laws, such as the *Employment Standards Act, 2000*, and the Ontario *Human Rights Code*, and their impact on hiring and employment practices.

- Understand a range of client retention strategies.

Advertising and Business Communications

Advertising Strategies

Advertising refers to conduct calculated to draw attention to a product or a business in order to encourage sales, generally through paid announcements in various media. All advertising by paralegals must not only be consistent with consumer protection laws, but also comply with Rules 2, 8.02, and 8.03 of the LSUC's *Paralegal Rules of Conduct*,[1] and Guideline 19 of the LSUC's *Paralegal Professional Conduct Guidelines*.[2]

In order to attract new clients and keep your business running, you will need to use advertising effectively. This will involve determining what form or forms of advertising is or are the most appropriate (based on your client and market profiles), what your advertising budget is, and what message you wish to convey.

The media you choose for advertising will depend partly on your budget, partly on the type of legal services you are offering, and partly on your targeted client base. For example, paralegals seeking to represent clients in criminal matters or provincial offences might consider advertising on benches located near courthouses or on buses that regularly stop outside those courthouses.

Your advertising budget will dictate to a large degree which media options are available to you. In theory, and historically, newspapers allow you to reach a wide audience relatively inexpensively, but there is no guarantee your ad will be seen, since newspapers are not usually read cover-to-cover if they are read in paper format. Furthermore, in the 21st century, newspaper circulation is not what it once was. While print newspapers may still be the best way to reach elderly prospective clients, younger clientele may be more accessible through online media. While advertising in a magazine or law report tailored to the legal profession such as the *Ontario Reports* is likely more expensive, your ad is more likely to be read by the audience of the publication. So, if you want to market to lawyers, legal trade publications are good media to use.

Radio spots can be effective and affordable ways to reach a broad cross-section of the population, but must be repeated often. Other affordable methods of advertising include sponsoring local sports teams, tournaments, and school fairs; posting ads on the boards of local arenas or on benches near bus shelters; and even advertising on the buses themselves. Using electronic media and maintaining a website are two important advertising methods today. Some legal services providers have blogs, while others regularly comment on professional social networking sites. Although sending out bulk emails is prohibited by the legislation informally known as Canada's

---

1   Law Society of Upper Canada, *Paralegal Rules of Conduct* (1 October 2014; amendments current to 2017), online: <https://www.lsuc.on.ca/paralegal-conduct-rules>.

2   Law Society of Upper Canada, *Paralegal Professional Conduct Guidelines* (1 October 2014; amendments current to 2016), online: <http://www.lsuc.on.ca/paralegal-conduct-guidelines>.

anti-spam legislation,[3] which amended laws such as the *Canadian Radio-television and Telecommunications Commission Act*,[4] the *Competition Act*,[5] and the *Personal Information Protection and Electronic Documents Act*,[6] the strategic use of comments and postings on search engines such as Google and professional social networking sites is an inexpensive way to help raise your profile.

Paralegals must be diligent in assessing all of their advertising in order to ensure compliance with Rules 8.02 and 8.03. Advertisements must not include deceptive or misleading statements, and must not omit any important information—for example, information regarding hidden fees and surcharges. With respect to hidden fees themselves, Guideline 13, section 9 discusses hidden fees and the importance of the relationship between client and paralegal. Guideline 13 explicitly states that the client must be able to rely on the paralegal's honesty and ability to act in the client's best interests, and prohibits paralegals from hiding financial dealings in the client's matter from the client.

Determining the message your ads will convey is an important decision. The claims you make should be realistic and credible. Choosing a single, consistent message that is easily understood and concise is often the best approach. A useful step in deciding where and how to allocate advertising funds is by testing what messages work. Researching the market and determining what competitors do and say in their advertising, and what works for them, will provide valuable insights. It may be worthwhile to obtain professional assistance.

In order to avoid lawsuits and to maintain the integrity of the profession, paralegals must also avoid making slanderous or libellous remarks against competitors in their advertising. It is also important for paralegals to adhere to copyright and trademark laws when designing business cards and letterhead, and creating slogans for their businesses.

Marketing

Maintaining a business inevitably involves marketing. **Marketing** is a broader concept than advertising; Rule 8.03 makes it clear that marketing includes advertising, but marketing generally also includes distribution, and selling, and involves disciplines as diverse as psychology, sociology, and economics. All interactions with clients and potential clients have an element of marketing. When you are providing services well, you are making a favourable impression and selling your business.

To develop and assess marketing—that is, to generate and refine ideas about how to promote your services—you can conduct market research. Information may be

marketing
a broader concept than advertising that focuses on branding, such as with the use of letterhead, business cards, and logos (Rule 8.03)

---

3   *An Act to promote the efficiency and adaptability of the Canadian economy by regulating certain activities that discourage reliance on electronic means of carrying out commercial activities, and to amend the Canadian Radio-television and Telecommunications Commission Act, the Competition Act, the Personal Information Protection and Electronic Documents Act and the Telecommunications Act*, SC 2010, c 23.

4   RSC 1985, c C-22.

5   RSC 1985, c C-34.

6   SC 2000, c 5.

gathered through the use of surveys or client evaluations, and research may be conducted either by the business or by third-party professionals. For example, you might provide a comments box in your waiting area, or give clients whose business is concluded an evaluation form asking them for feedback; you might ask about their level of satisfaction and any suggestions for improvement. It is preferable that your clients bring their complaints to you, rather than to other potential clients or the LSUC.

A marketing strategy is an important part of a business's overall business plan. **Strategic planning** refers to a process that takes place annually in many organizations. Key players within the business assess the current business situation and the environment and determine whether they are changing. This is a time when you can reflect on new trends and opportunities in order to take advantage of them and avoid any negative consequences, such as loss of client base. Your business plan can be fine-tuned (or even altered dramatically) to respond to changes as they unfold. Stepping back from day-to-day operational concerns and putting your mind to the bigger picture and future opportunities is key to the success of your business.

strategic planning
the process of assessing the current business situation and the environment to determine whether they are changing, and revising the business plans to reflect the findings

Business Communications

Still broader than the concept of marketing is **business communication**, which encompasses marketing, customer relations, branding, community engagement, advertising, public relations, and employee management. Business communication includes internal communication between employees as well as external communication with clients or the public. Communication skills are extremely important for paralegals and extend to written communication, which should, as far as possible, appear professional and conform to spelling and grammatical rules.

business communication
communication for the purpose of carrying out business activities; includes marketing, customer relations, branding, community engagement, advertising, public relations, and employee management

> Interestingly, in an article discussing "scooping" by a Toronto lawyer specializing in criminal law, noted columnist Christie Blatchford spent a fair bit of time discussing the spelling and grammatical errors contained in a letter written by that lawyer. That letter attempted to solicit as a client someone who had been charged with murder and who was already represented. It is also interesting that the letter had initially been posted on a listserve for members of the Criminal Lawyers' Association.

The expanding range of telecommunications technologies has broadened the scope of communications available to businesses. While communicating in person—and through print, radio, and television media—remains important, businesses increasingly communicate using email, websites, and online professional social networking media.

Because external communication shapes your business's brand and public image, controlling this type of communication is critical. Damage done to your business's public image is difficult to repair, and having policies regarding who may speak for the enterprise—particularly to the media—is sound practice. Your business may be responsible for communications made on its behalf by anyone acting as its agent, whether the person is an employee, a spokesperson, or even someone who only *seems* to be a spokesperson, such as a relative. Liability can include civil damages, regulatory or statutory liability, as well as accountability to the LSUC.

Rules 2.01 and 8, and Guideline 19

In addition to the restrictions on advertising that apply to all businesses, lawyers and paralegals must know and observe the restrictions imposed by the LSUC.

Rule 2.01 requires paralegals to conduct themselves in a manner that maintains the integrity of the paralegal profession. This obligation is extremely broad, and allows the LSUC to revoke licences for a wide range of conduct that it deems inappropriate. Because of its visibility, advertising may be given a particularly high level of scrutiny by the LSUC.

Rule 8 deals with issues related to practice management, including general obligations, advertising, insurance, firm names, letterhead, and signs.

Under Rule 8.02(2), paralegals are required to make legal services available to the public in an efficient and convenient way, and in doing so may not use means

(a) that are false or misleading;

(b) that amount to coercion, duress, or harassment;

(c) that take advantage of a person who is vulnerable or who has suffered a traumatic experience and has not yet had a chance to recover (a practice known as "ambulance chasing");

(d) that are intended to influence a person who has retained another paralegal or lawyer for a particular matter to change his or her representative for that matter [a practice known as "poaching" or "scooping"], unless the change is initiated by the person or the other representative; or

(e) that otherwise bring the paralegal profession or the administration of justice into disrepute.

Rule 8.02(2)(e) means that the LSUC can sanction paralegals for conduct it deems to be distasteful even if they did not breach any particular rule in their advertising practices; in other words, paralegals must comply not only with the "letter" of the Rules but with their "spirit." Paralegals are also prohibited from advertising services that are beyond the permitted scope of practice for paralegals, such as real estate (Rule 8.02(3)).

With respect to vulnerable persons or people who have suffered traumatic experiences, Guideline 19, section 2 provides some clarification of the Rule discussed above:

A person who is vulnerable or who has suffered a traumatic experience and has not yet had a chance to recover may need the professional assistance of a paralegal. A paralegal is permitted to provide assistance to a person if a close relative or personal friend of the person contacts the paralegal for this purpose, and to offer assistance to a person with whom the paralegal has a close family or professional relationship. Rules 8.02 and 8.03 prohibit the paralegal from using unconscionable or exploitive or other means that bring the profession or the administration of justice into disrepute.

Furthermore, section 4 of Guideline 19 provides as follows:

Rules 8.02 and 8.03 impose certain restrictions and obligations on a paralegal who wishes to market and/or advertise his or her legal services. The *Rules* help to ensure that a paralegal does not mislead clients or the public while still permitting the paralegal to differentiate himself or herself and his or her services from those of lawyers or other paralegals. A paralegal should ensure that his or her marketing and advertising does not suggest that the paralegal is a lawyer and should take steps to correct any misapprehension on the part of a client or prospective client in that respect.

In *Law Society of Upper Canada v Cao*, 2016 ONLSTH 116, in an agreed statement of facts the paralegal admitted to having engaged in professional misconduct by practising outside the scope of practice and using misleading business cards. In that case, the paralegal appeared as a representative in a "super summary" conviction matter where the penalty for the charge was more than six months' imprisonment. The judicial pre-trial judge in the super summary conviction matter, concerned about the paralegal's competency, asked to see his business card and believed it to be misleading, since it did not state that Mr. Cao was a paralegal, but gave the impression that he was a lawyer. As a result, the associate chief justice made a complaint to the LSUC.

Rule 8.03 addresses marketing, and provides that the term "marketing" includes advertisements and other similar communications in various media, and includes firm names (including trade names), letterhead, business cards, and logos. Paralegals may market legal services if the marketing

    (a) is demonstrably true, accurate, and verifiable;

    (b) is neither misleading, confusing, or deceptive, nor likely to mislead, confuse, or deceive; and

    (c) is in the best interests of the public and is consistent with a high standard of professionalism.

This rule also addresses the advertising of fees, and provides that fees may be advertised if

    (a) the advertising is reasonably precise as to the services offered for each fee quoted;

    (b) the advertising states whether other amounts, such as disbursements and taxes, will be charged in addition to the fee; and

    (c) the paralegal adheres to the advertised fee.

Like Rule 8.02, the limits imposed by Rule 8.03 are broadly framed—for example, paralegals may only use marketing that is "true, accurate and verifiable," that is not "misleading," and that is "consistent with a high standard of professionalism." In cases where you are unsure whether or not the LSUC would approve of a particular advertising, marketing, or fees strategy, you may wish to err on the side of caution. The statements in the Rules and the Guidelines are meant to complement—not serve as substitutes for—paralegals' professional judgment. In the case of *Law Society of Upper Canada v Zappia, infra*, it is interesting to note that the LSUC obtained legal opinions from external counsel in order to assist it in determining whether the advertising in question breached the Rules concerning advertising of contingency fees. The panel specifically commented that the "uncertainty around these particular Rules was costly to both parties" and went on to say that "the work undertaken by the Society [LSUC] and Mr. Zappia will be of benefit to the profession at large."

Section 5 of Guideline 19 provides examples of marketing practices that may violate Rule 8.03(1):

(a) stating an amount of money that the paralegal has recovered for a client or referring to the paralegal's degree of success in past cases, unless such statement is accompanied by a further statement that past results are not necessarily indicative of future results and that the amount recovered and other litigation outcomes will vary according to the facts in individual cases;

(b) suggesting qualitative superiority to lawyers or other paralegals;

(c) raising expectations;

(d) suggesting or implying that the paralegal is aggressive;

(e) disparaging or demeaning other persons, groups, organizations, or institutions; and

(f) using testimonials or endorsements that contain emotional appeals.

Section 6 of Guideline 19 provides examples of marketing practices that do contravene Rule 8.03(1):

(a) marketing services that the paralegal is not currently able to perform to the standard of a competent paralegal;

(b) bait-and-switch marketing, which attracts clients by offers of services, prices, or terms different from those commonly provided to clients who respond to the marketing;

(c) marketing that fails to clearly and prominently disclose a practice that the paralegal has of referring clients for a fee, or other consideration, to other licensees;

(d) failing to expressly state that the marketed services will be provided by licensed lawyers, by licensed paralegals, or by both; and

(e) referring to awards, rankings, and third-party endorsements that are not bona fide or that are likely to be misleading, confusing, or deceptive.

Section 7 of Guideline 19 indicates that the Rule's requirements apply to different forms of marketing, including advertisements about the size, location, and nature of the paralegal's practice and awards and endorsements from third parties.

Section 8 of Guideline 19 clearly states that the intention behind the first four prohibitions is to ensure that marketing does not mislead by failing to make clear what services are actually available and are intended to be provided.

Section 9 of that guideline provides additional information concerning those awards, rankings, and third-party endorsements, stating that they are intended to be interpreted broadly and will include terms such as "best," "super," "#1," and similar terms. The rule will be contravened where the awards, rankings, and third-party endorsements do not genuinely reflect the performance of the paralegal and the quality of service provided by that paralegal yet appear to do so. The rule will also be contravened where these awards, rankings, and third-party endorsements are not the result of a reasonable evaluative process, but are conferred, in part, as a result of the payment of a fee or other consideration rather than as a result of a legitimate evaluation of the performance and quality of a paralegal. In addition, if, at the time of reference, the paralegal could not have demonstrated that the awards or rankings complied with the rule, that will constitute a breach of the rule.

Section 10 of Guideline 19 indicates that particular care should be taken in respect of awards and rankings referenced in mass advertising, such as in newspaper and Internet advertising, television advertising, and advertising on buses, billboards, and taxis. In that situation the paralegal is obliged to be careful to ensure that the references to awards, rankings, and third-party endorsements are particularly clear and straightforward.

Section 11 of Guideline 19 indicates that references to awards and honours that are genuine reflections of the professional or civic service do not contravene this rule. Examples cited in the section include LSUC awards.

Other sections of Guideline 19 require marketing practices to comply with human rights laws in Ontario and to be consistent with a high standard of professionalism.

> In *Law Society of Upper Canada v Zappia*, 2015 ONLSTH 34, in an agreed statement of facts a paralegal admitted to professional misconduct for misleading advertising, for an ad on his website that said "We Win or It's Free." In fact, a non-refundable administrative fee was charged. In addition, the advertising of contingency fees was made with respect to quasi-criminal matters, where such fee arrangements are prohibited. Interestingly, in this case all of the complaints to the LSUC were made by other paralegals—no clients complained to the LSUC.

In February 2017, the Professional Regulation Committee presented to the LSUC a report that included the report of the Advertisements & Fee Arrangements Issues Working Group concerning lawyers' and paralegals' advertising. That report has already resulted in amendments to the Rules governing paralegals' marketing. In particular, Rule 8.03 now includes subsections (4) and (5), which provide as follows:

(4) A paralegal marketing legal services shall specifically identify in all marketing materials that he or she is licensed as a paralegal.

(5) The marketing of second opinion services is prohibited.

In a bulletin to licensees, the LSUC advised that the purpose of requiring licensees to identify in their advertising whether they are a lawyer or a paralegal is to "enhance the public's awareness of the different types of licences and to help the public make a more informed choice of legal service provider."

Second opinion services may still be provided, but advertising those services is no longer permitted. Section 15 of Guideline 19 makes it clear that although the provision of second opinions is a valuable service to clients, second opinion marketing is commonly done with a view to obtaining the retainer, rather than providing a second opinion. It explicitly refers to this practice as "bait and switch" marketing.

Letterhead and Signs

The limits on marketing set out in Rule 8.03 also apply to the way in which paralegals may identify themselves on signs, letterhead, business cards, and logos—that is, any information that these items contain must be true, accurate, verifiable, and so on. For example, the letterhead of a paralegal sole proprietor should not say "and partners"; limited liability partnerships and professional corporations must identify themselves as such (see the discussion in Chapter 3).

Letterheads and signs should not be profane or glib. Certain kinds of catchy and comedic slogans, signs, and logos would not be in keeping with the high standard of professionalism required by the Rules.

Setting Fees

For paralegals in Ontario, determining what fees to charge for their services is both a business management and a regulatory compliance issue. In setting appropriate fees, paralegals must respond to market demands as well as observe the limitations imposed by the LSUC.

Business Considerations—Fees

As section 2 of Guideline 13 states, a fee is the paralegal's wage. Fees may be hourly, by stages of a matter, or fixed or flat, or, with some restrictions, they may be contingency fees (discussed in more detail under the subheading "Contingency Fees"). In general, paralegal entrepreneurs must set their fees at a level where they can, by working a reasonable number of hours, cover their costs and earn a profit. Setting fees is a matter of individual strategy on the part of a business, and while conventional economic wisdom suggests that businesses should market their services at a price level that is similar to that of their competitors, there are a number of things you should keep in mind when setting fees.

A good preliminary strategy is determining what "cost-based prices" would be. These are fees that reflect what it costs your business to stay in business.[8] You should periodically assess and reassess the costs you incur in the course of providing your services to determine the total cost of operating your business. Among the expenditures you should consider are overhead, payroll, and materials; these costs are often underestimated. You should also consider office expenses (such as rent, electric bills,

---

8 Daniel P Dern, "How to Set Prices for Your Services: A Step by Step Guide to Calculating What You Must—or CAN—Charge" (1997), online: <http://www.dern.com/hw2price.shtml>.

postage, and telephone and Internet bills), professional licensing fees, insurance, and any other memberships and/or subscriptions incidental to your business.

Once you have determined a cost-based amount for your services, you should keep in mind that there is a good deal of psychological subtlety involved in the business practice of setting final fees. Although the lowest prices may attract more clients in certain business areas, where professional services—and legal services in particular—are concerned, clients may not wish to retain a "bargain basement" paralegal. There is also the question of what value a legal services provider's expertise, education, and experience have in the market. You may wish to look into what other comparable organizations or sole proprietors are charging for similar legal services.

Another aspect of setting appropriate fees is managing client expectations. As section 1 of Guideline 13 states,

> Too often, misunderstandings about fees and disbursements result in disputes over legal bills and complaints from unhappy clients. Since these disputes reflect badly on the paralegal profession and the administration of justice, it is important that a paralegal discuss with his or her client(s) the amount of fees and disbursements that will likely be charged. It will be to the benefit of all concerned if the paralegal ensures that the client has a clear understanding not only of what legal services the paralegal will provide, but how much those services are likely to cost.

When you enter into a retainer agreement, you should review the details of the retainer agreement with the client. The fees that the client can expect to pay and when he or she will be required to pay them should be made very clear, and a schedule of fees should be provided to the client in writing. Keeping existing clients and gaining new ones through referrals depends largely on how well you manage your clients' expectations. In order for your clients to feel satisfied with the legal services they are receiving from you, the financial arrangements must be completely transparent. For further discussion of retainer agreements and a sample retainer agreement, refer to Chapter 6.

Fee collection is a common problem faced by practitioners. It is important to ensure that your retainer is replenished as needed, and that you do not invest many hours in a matter only to face non-payment of your invoice. In order to reduce the possibility of misunderstanding or surprise, you should bill your clients regularly and frequently. Your clients may not realize how quickly legal fees can grow to an unanticipated size.

> Even established law firms are not immune to the issue of non-payment of fees. In *Hillsburg Stables Inc v Gardiner Roberts LLP*, 2012 ONCA 95, the law firm Gardiner Roberts LLP was owed in excess of $800,000 in unpaid accounts (fees and disbursements). This case deals with the firm's attempt to enforce security it was granted in order to collect those unpaid fees and disbursements.
>
> Note that the appellant's name is spelled incorrectly in the CanLII citation. The correct spelling is Hillsburgh Stables Inc.

One way you can deal with this problem is to accept credit card payments, since this transfers the responsibility for debt collection onto credit card companies. Despite the monthly fees you will pay for this service, it may be a worthwhile investment.

LSUC Rules—Fees

Beyond the general business management considerations discussed above, Rule 5 imposes additional constraints on the fees that paralegals may charge.

Rule 5.01(1) provides that all fees and disbursements charged or accepted by paralegals should be fair and reasonable, and must have been disclosed in a timely manner. What is fair and reasonable will depend on factors such as the following (Rule 5.01(2)):

(a) the time and effort required and spent;

(b) the difficulty and importance of the matter;

(c) whether special skill or service was required and provided;

(d) the amount involved or the value of the subject matter;

(e) the results obtained;

(f) fees authorized by statute or regulation; and

(g) special circumstances.

Clients must be informed promptly and provided with specific details regarding fees charged. In addition, section 6 of Guideline 13 makes it clear that paralegals should provide clients with as much information as possible concerning fees, disbursements, and interest and should provide that information in writing prior to or within a reasonable time after commencing representation. Section 7 of Guideline 13 explicitly states that paralegals should not manipulate fees and disbursements in a manner to provide a lower fee estimate. Section 8 of that guideline discusses unexpected costs that are higher than the paralegal's initial estimate and indicates that when unexpected costs are incurred the paralegal should give the client a revised estimate together with an explanation as to why the original estimate has changed. Once the client has received that estimate and provided instructions to the paralegal, the paralegal is to confirm the new understanding in writing.

According to Rule 5.01(3), paralegals may not accept compensation related to their employment from anyone other than the client, except in cases where they have made full disclosure regarding the arrangement to the client and have obtained the client's consent. This protects clients against a conflict of interest in the event that the interests of the person paying your fee and the interests of your client diverge.

Disbursements are amounts for out-of-pocket expenses relating to a particular file, such as photocopies, postage, long-distance telephone charges, and court filing fees. Section 4 of Guideline 13 lists several common disbursements. You may seek reimbursement for these costs from your client, but you must clearly set them apart from the fee portion of your bill in a statement of account (Rule 5.01(4)). In addition, section 5 of Guideline 13 clearly states that a paralegal cannot profit from disbursements and may only charge clients the actual disbursement costs. Paralegals may not disburse overhead costs, such as rent.

Paralegals are routinely required to hold money in trust—for example, they hold retainer funds in trust prior to providing their services. Very strict rules apply to funds held in trust, including the fact that they must be kept separate and apart in a trust account. Paralegals may only withdraw funds from their trust accounts in circumstances set out in the Rules—for example, to pay for legal services rendered, and in this case only after the client has been billed. These obligations will be discussed in greater detail in Chapter 7.

Referral Fees

A referral is the act of suggesting the name of another paralegal or lawyer to a client when the work is not done through the firm in which the referring paralegal primarily practises. Guideline 13, section 13 explains that a **referral fee** is "a fee paid by a paralegal to another paralegal or lawyer for referring a client to the paralegal," or "a fee paid to the paralegal by another paralegal or lawyer for his or her referral of a client to the other paralegal or lawyer."

In April 2017, the Rules concerning referral fees were amended. According to Rule 5.01(15), which applies to **referral agreements** entered into after April 27, 2017, and to situations in which no enforceable referral agreement was entered into prior to or on April 27, 2017, paralegals may receive a referral fee from another licensee for referring a client if

- the referral was not made because of a conflict of interest;
- the referral was not made because the paralegal or lawyer's licence was suspended at the time of the referral;
- the fee is reasonable and does not increase the total amount of the fee payable by the client;
- a referral agreement was entered into at the time of the referral or as soon as practicable after the referral; and
- the paralegal or lawyer who receives the referral has the expertise and ability to handle the matter.

Rule 5.01(15)(e) caps the amount of the referral fee. The rule provides that the amount of the referral fee should not exceed 15 percent of the fees paid to the paralegal or lawyer who received the referral for the first $50,000 of such fees for the matter and 5 percent of any additional fees for the matter to a maximum referral fee of $25,000.

Rule 5.01(17) indicates that for matters where referral fees are being paid pursuant to enforceable agreements to pay and receive referral fees made prior to or on April 27, 2017, the relevant considerations are as follows:

(a) the fee is reasonable and does not increase the total amount of the fee charged to the client; and

(b) the client is informed and consents.

If the agreement was unwritten, Rule 5.01(18) provides that the paralegal who is entitled to receive fees should confirm the agreement in writing to the other party to the agreement as soon as is practicable and requires the client to be provided with a copy of the confirmation.

Rule 5.01(14) indicates that the referral agreement required by Rule 5.01(15) is a signed written agreement between the referring paralegal or lawyer, the licensee to

referral fee
a fee paid by a paralegal to another paralegal or lawyer for referring a client to the paralegal, or a fee paid to the paralegal by another paralegal or lawyer for his or her referral of a person to another paralegal or lawyer

referral agreement
a signed written agreement between the referring paralegal or lawyer, the licensee to whom the client is referred, and the client being referred; the agreement must be in the form provided by the LSUC

whom the client is referred, and the client being referred. The agreement must be in the form provided by the LSUC, and include the following:

(a) confirmation that the client has been advised and understands that the client has no obligation to accept the referral;

(b) confirmation that the client has been provided with information about the Law Society's requirements for payment and receipt of referral fees and a reasonable opportunity to review and consider that information;

(c) confirmation that the referring paralegal or lawyer has recommended at least two paralegals or lawyers to the client and, if not, disclosure of the reason that it has not been reasonably possible to do so;

(d) a provision that the client is free to retain a paralegal or lawyer other than the one who receives the referral;

(e) the reason(s) that the referring paralegal or lawyer has recommended the specific referee to the client;

(f) full and fair disclosure of the relationship between the referring paralegal or lawyer and the paralegal or lawyer who receives the referral;

(g) confirmation that no referral fee will be paid or payable unless and until the paralegal or lawyer who receives the referral is paid his or her fee for legal services for the matter; and

(h) full and fair disclosure of the referral fee including the circumstances in which the referral fee is payable and the basis upon which the amount of the referral fee is determined.

See the LSUC's Standard Referral Fee Agreement reproduced in Appendix 5.1 to this chapter.

Paralegals sometimes give and receive referrals to and from colleagues who are practising in different areas of law. Many do not charge a fee for such referrals, with the expectation that their colleagues will do the same. In addition, section 14 of Guideline 13 makes it clear that certain arrangements are not prohibited by the Rules:

(a) making an arrangement respecting the purchase and sale of a professional business when the consideration payable includes a percentage of revenues generated from the business sold;

(b) entering into a lease under which a landlord directly or indirectly shares in the fees or revenues generated by the provision of legal services; and

(c) paying an employee for services, other than for referring clients, based on the revenue of the paralegal's firm or professional business.

Fee Splitting

Section 12 of Guideline 13 defines fee splitting as follows: **Fee splitting** occurs when a paralegal shares or divides his or her fee with another person. According to Rule 5.01(12), paralegals may not split fees. Specifically, they should not

fee splitting
occurs when a paralegal shares or divides his or her fee with another person

(a) directly or indirectly share, split, or divide their fees with any person who is not a licensee, including an affiliated entity; or

 (b) give any financial or other reward to any person who is not a licensee, including an affiliated entity for the referral of clients or client matters.

An exception is made where a paralegal is operating in a multi-discipline practice with non-licensee partners where the partnership agreement provides for the sharing of fees, cash flows, or profits among members of the firm (Rule 5.01(13)).

The provisions above mean that paralegals may not refer business to other institutions or service providers—such as banks, accountants, or investment advisers—*for a fee*. It does not prohibit them from making referrals where no fee is involved, or prohibit non-licensees from working in multi-discipline practices with other kinds of professionals, such as accountants and investment advisers.

Contingency Fees

contingency fee
a fee paid based on a percentage of the final settlement or judgment, and therefore payable only if the client is successful

Contingency fees are fees that are paid depending on the outcome of a case. Where a case is unsuccessful, no fee is charged. If damages are awarded or successfully negotiated on behalf of your client, you are paid based on a predetermined percentage of the damages amount rather than according to an hourly rate or specified task amount.

Except in criminal or quasi-criminal matters (see *Law Society of Upper Canada v Zappia*, above), Rule 5 permits paralegals to enter into agreements where their fee is contingent on the successful completion of a matter. An agreement for remuneration by contingency fee must be in writing, and the paralegal must explain to the client the factors that are being used to determine the percentage or other basis of payment, including

- the likelihood of success,
- the nature and complexity of the claim,
- the expense and risk of pursuing it,
- the amount of the expected recovery,
- who is to receive an award of costs, and
- the amount of costs awarded.

Section 24 of Guideline 13 makes it clear that even when these factors are considered, contingency fees must be fair and reasonable. Section 25 of that guideline states that the contingency fee agreement with respect to the method for calculating contingency fees should be clear. Section 26 of the guideline refers paralegals to O Reg 195/04 to the *Solicitor's Act*[9] for guidance as to what matters are to be included in a contingency fee agreement, although that legislation, and this particular regulation, governs lawyers rather than paralegals.

Contingency fees may account for part or all of a paralegal's payment for a particular matter. The following scenario deals with a situation in which a licensee decides to accept a retainer on a contingency fee basis.

---

9 RSO 1990, c S.15.

Contingency Planning

Aaron Romero graduated from a paralegal training program in 2013. Immediately upon obtaining his licence, he started his own practice and was eager to take on clients.

In an effort to build his clientele, he started advertising his services for small claims and highway traffic offences on a popular online classifieds site. His ads touted only his knowledge in these areas of practice and his strong litigation skills. There were no gimmicks, punchy slogans, or special offers.

He received numerous responses. Some were from people seriously seeking out representation. Others were from those just looking to get free legal advice.

Aaron scheduled roughly eight consultations a week from his online ads. He took great care during those meetings to listen to what the potential client had to say, thoroughly review all the documents, and give an honest and frank assessment of each case.

With each consultation, he was confident he was fully knowledgeable and competent to properly represent the client in resolving his or her matter.

Then discussion turned to fees and payment, which he found was a source of great frustration.

When he built his business plan, he set his fee at $75 an hour, which he believed was a fair rate for his skills and experience, having worked in a law firm assisting lawyers prior to pursuing his paralegal career.

During one consultation, he met with Beverley, a woman who wanted to file a small claims lawsuit against the company that contracted her to provide cleaning services for its shop. She claimed the company had unilaterally changed the terms of the contract and failed to pay invoices for the services she had provided.

Based on their discussions, Aaron quoted her a $1,500 retainer for the case. The client felt the amount was fair, but perhaps encouraged by advertisements from other lawyers and paralegals claiming "we don't get paid unless you get paid," the client wanted to pay the fees on a contingency basis.

Aaron didn't like the idea of working on a contingency basis. He feared he would be stuck chasing clients for payment and defending his work in the process, particularly if clients were disappointed they did not get everything they asked for in their matters.

But it was early on in his career and he needed clients; he found that a significant number of the potential clients who came to him by way of his advertisements wanted this kind of contingency arrangement.

Based on the documents and details provides, Aaron was sufficiently confident that he could win Beverley's case, so he agreed to work on a partial contingency basis. He would take a $500 retainer to prepare and file the pleadings and prepare for the mandatory settlement conference. He would bill the rest when the case was successfully resolved.

The case was resolved in settlement conference, and Aaron was fully paid a reduced rate, since no trial was needed.

What would you do when a client wants to pay on contingency? Would you take the risk or decline the retainer?

Hiring Employees

Choosing the right employees is critical to the success of your business. You may wish to advertise available positions on the LSUC website or in publications such as the *Ontario Reports*, as well as in newspapers and other online job sites. Most positions are filled by word of mouth, and this is another reason why communicating with colleagues and former classmates is a good idea. When interviewing potential employees, ask questions that will allow you to determine whether particular candidates are competent, trustworthy, and would be a good fit for your organization. Always check references carefully; finding out that a particular individual would not be an asset to your business before—rather than after—you hire him or her will save you time and money later.

Rule 2.03 and the Ontario *Human Rights Code*[10] prohibit discrimination against employees and prospective employees on any of the following grounds: race, ancestry, place of origin, colour, ethnic origin, citizenship, creed, sex, sexual orientation, age, record of offences, marital status, family status, disability, gender identity, or gender expression. It is your responsibility to ensure that your recruiting methods do not violate human rights. Examples of unacceptable practices would include advertising a position for a "young graduate" or a "Canadian citizen" and asking candidates in an interview whether they intend to have children within the next few years.

Even if you do not intend to discriminate, you should be aware that practices such as those just described are prohibited and could lead to complaints against you to a human rights tribunal or the LSUC. Paralegals are responsible for finding out what kinds of accommodations they may be required to make for their employees—for example, accommodating an employee or prospective employee with a physical disability by building a wheelchair ramp or providing special computer equipment or chairs. You should consult the Ontario Human Rights Commission to find out what your specific obligations in certain situations are.

The *Employment Standards Act, 2000*[11] governs working conditions for non-union employees and covers things such as minimum wage, overtime, breaks, leaves of absence, vacation, and termination pay. Before you begin hiring employees for your business, you should be familiar with your obligations in these areas; information is available on the Ontario Ministry of Labour website. Note that with regard to the termination of employees, common law obligations expand on the minimum notice requirements of the Act where there is no employment contract. To protect yourself against wrongful dismissal lawsuits, it is good practice to have written employment contracts that set out specific notice periods.

Before hiring anyone, you must obtain a business number from the Canada Revenue Agency (CRA) and open a payroll deductions account. Deductions for income tax must be made from the employee's pay and held in trust in this account until they are remitted to the CRA. You may also be required to deduct amounts for the Canada Pension Plan and for Employment Insurance. Failure to deduct, report, or remit these sums to the CRA can result in fines ranging between $1,000 and $25,000 and/or a term of imprisonment of up to 12 months.

---

10   RSO 1990, c H.19.

11   SO 2000, c 41.

The *Occupational Health and Safety Act*[12] outlines the rights and duties of various parties in the workplace in order to protect workers from health and safety hazards, while the *Workplace Safety and Insurance Act, 1997*[13] governs compensation for workplace injuries and diseases. Your obligations under these statutes may depend on the size of your workforce. You may have taken an employment law course in college, and reviewing your notes before you begin hiring employees will serve you well.

Employee Handbooks

Although employers are under no legal or regulatory obligation to develop an employee handbook, doing so is smart business practice. Employee handbooks detail the organization's mission, policies, and procedures. Because paralegals are responsible for the actions and omissions of their employees, the handbook should reference the Rules, especially those relating to client confidentiality and file storage. Employee handbooks may also include your policies regarding sexual harassment, dress codes, computer usage, scheduling, parking, smoking, discipline procedures, and other work rules. Procedures for specific work tasks may be outlined in detail.

Employees should be given their handbooks on their first day of work and should be required to sign an acknowledgment that they have understood their contents and obligations. This can prevent misunderstandings and conflicts. Ensure that your employees understand that the handbook is *not* part of their employment contract and that you may amend it at any time. Remember to schedule time to regularly review the manual to determine whether updates are required.

Client Retention Strategies

Advertising and marketing strategies can attract clients to your business, but maintaining relationships with existing clients is often the key to business success. In the legal services business, many client relationships are long term, particularly where the legal services being provided relate to businesses. This is one reason why retaining clients is extremely important. In addition, existing clients can help promote your business, since informal personal referrals remain an important way for legal services providers to attract new clients.

The better your relationships with your clients are, the more likely you are to retain clients and receive referrals. The skills necessary to build better client relationships can be learned and honed, beginning with building trust. To do this, you need to cultivate habits and styles that will convey your credibility, competence, and integrity. The following are five things you can do to help strengthen your relationships with your clients.

Be Interested

Make small talk. Talk *with* clients and coworkers rather than *at* them. Try to remember details about their lives. It may be helpful to keep notes attached to client files and to review them briefly before speaking with clients. Set aside time each week to

---

12   RSO 1990, c O.1.
13   SO 1997, c 16, Schedule A.

connect with existing clients without an urgent reason to do so. Check in with them to see how they are doing, and what their current goals and interests are. Conveying empathy and "going where the client goes" will help nurture relationships.[14]

Dress Appropriately

The way you present yourself to others is an important aspect of non-verbal communication. Your image and reputation can be shaped by simple habits, such as by wearing clean clothing that fits well and that helps you project confidence. Clients tend to seek legal advice from individuals who look the part—that is, who look more conservative. You should also consider what other messages the way you present yourself might be sending to others. Flashy displays of wealth might be off-putting to some clients, while if you are seeking work from "green" companies you should be mindful of how your attire reflects your attitudes in this regard.

Be Respectful

Many people view legal services providers as arrogant and self-involved. Respecting your clients' time will help foster trust, especially when your currency is the billable hour. Don't keep people waiting. Don't be late. Focus your attention entirely on clients when speaking to them. Turn off your telephone, computer, or smartphone during client meetings. Return client messages promptly; failure to return telephone calls is one of the most common complaints against lawyers and paralegals.

Showcase Your Knowledge—Appropriately

If you are working with others, promote the solid team of competent professionals who work with you. If you are a sole practitioner, promote your extensive network of colleagues, your competence, and your confidence. Display your credentials, such as by hanging your diploma and certificates on your office wall.

Be sensitive to clients' individual needs and tailor your approach. Some clients may not appreciate small talk (especially if you are charging by the hour), so make it clear that you do not charge for small talk. Other clients may wish to share, even if it's just to vent, and will appreciate that you take the time to listen. Make sure to ask your clients what they want to know, and assure them that you have the expertise and experience required to represent them if indeed you do. If you are not competent to handle a matter, be honest with the client and seek assistance, or refer the client to a lawyer or another paralegal. This will enhance rather than detract from your reputation, and will likely generate reciprocal referrals.

Be Involved

As your business gets busier, you may be tempted to reduce your involvement in volunteer activities or professional groups. When considering how to balance various demands on your time, keep in mind that the investment in professional and non-profit organizations will pay dividends in the form of high levels of visibility, support networks, and—ultimately—referrals. Establish yourself as an expert among experts.

---

14 For more information on creating trust with clients, see Charles H Green, "Create Trust, Gain a Client" (2009), online: <http://trustedadvisor.com/articles/create-trust-gain-a-client>.

Building your "you" brand will help you attract new clients, retain existing ones, and minimize the risk of complaints against you to the LSUC. Your demeanour and conduct should be priorities. Failure to conduct yourself with candour, honesty, and professionalism could lead to the loss of your licence and the end of your business.

Conclusion

In their advertising and marketing, paralegals must observe consumer protection laws as well as the Rules imposed by the LSUC. The general provision in the Rules that requires paralegals to conduct themselves in a manner that maintains the integrity of the paralegal profession extends to advertising and marketing.

Marketing includes advertisements and other similar communications in various media, as well as firm names (including trade names), letterhead, business cards, and logos. You must ensure that your ads do not omit any important information, and that they do not contain deceptive or misleading statements, or slanderous or libellous remarks against competitors. All marketing must be demonstrably true, accurate, and verifiable, and be consistent with a high standard of professionalism. When advertising fees, the advertising with respect to the services offered for each fee quoted must be reasonably precise, and must not contain hidden fees and surcharges, and the paralegal must adhere to the fee.

The Rules regarding advertising and marketing are broadly framed. Where you are unsure whether or not the LSUC would approve of a particular advertising, marketing, or fees strategy, you may wish to err on the side of caution.

Controlling external communication is critical to preserving your business's public image and reputation. You may be responsible for communications made on behalf of your business by anyone acting as its agent, and liability may include civil damages, regulatory or statutory liability, as well as accountability to the LSUC.

A good starting point when setting fees is to determine a cost-based amount for your services, and then to decide what would be reasonable based on your education, experience, and expertise—and to consider what other comparable businesses are charging for similar legal services. You must also observe provisions in the Rules governing fees and disbursements, referral fees, fee splitting, and contingency fees.

Before you begin hiring employees for your business, you should be familiar with your obligations under the *Human Rights Code* and various employment legislation, including the *Employment Standards Act, 2000*, the *Occupational Health and Safety Act*, and the *Workplace Safety and Insurance Act, 1997*. You must also obtain a business number from the CRA and open a payroll deductions account.

Strong, long-term client relationships built on a foundation of trust are essential to the success of your business. In addition to providing repeat business, existing clients can be a source of personal referrals. You can build better client relationships and retain clients by being interested in them as individuals beyond your immediate business relationship with them, by presenting a professional image, by treating them with respect, by displaying your professional knowledge and competence appropriately, and by becoming and staying involved with volunteer activities and professional groups throughout your career.

APPENDIX 5.1

Standard Referral Fee Agreement

LAW SOCIETY OF UPPER CANADA

REFERRAL AGREEMENT

This **Referral Agreement** confirms the referral by [Referrer Name] of [Client Name] to [Referree Name] and the related referral fee payment terms.

REFERRAL RECOMMENDATION:

[Client Name] wishes to obtain legal services with respect to [briefly describe the legal matter].

[Referrer Name] has recommended [Referree Name] to [Client Name] because [reasons for referral].

ADD IF there is a relationship between the Referrer and the Referree:

[Referrer Name] has disclosed to [Client Name] that [Referrer Name] and [Referree Name] have the following relationship: [describe any legal, financial or other relationship between Referrer and Referree].

[Referrer Name] also recommended the following [lawyers and/or paralegals] to [Client Name]: [names].

OR

It has not been reasonably possible for [Referrer Name] to recommend any other [lawyer(s) or paralegal(s)] to [Client Name] because [reasons for not providing other names].

EXPLANATION OF REFERRAL FEES AND CLIENT RIGHTS:

[Client Name] has been provided with the **Law Society's Requirements for Referral Fees** (attached). [Client Name] has had the opportunity to review and consider the requirements.

[Client Name] has been advised and understands that there is **no obligation to retain** [Referree Name] or any other [lawyer or paralegal] referred by [Referrer Name]. [Client Name] is free to retain another [lawyer or paralegal] of his/her choice.

After signing this Referral Agreement, [Client Name] understands that [Client Name] has the **right to terminate the retainer with [Referree Name]** at any time and for any reason.

[Client Name] has no obligation either to [Referrer Name] or [Referree Name] as a result of this Referral Agreement.

ACCEPTANCE OF REFERRAL AND REFERRAL FEE PAYMENT TERMS:

[Client Name] has accepted the referral to [Referree Name].

For this referral, [Referree Name] agrees to pay [Referrer Name] a referral fee:

- in the amount of [insert set dollar value];

OR

- in an amount equal to [Percentage%] of the fees paid by [Client Name] to [Referree Name] for the legal matter referred;

OR

- [such other basis as may be agreed]

In any event, the referral fee will not exceed the amount permitted by the *Rules of Professional Conduct* or the *Paralegal Rules of Conduct*. A sample calculation is set out in the Law Society's Requirements for Referral Fees.

This referral fee will not be paid or payable until [Referree Name] is paid his or her fees in the matter.

The referral fee will be noted on the account sent to [Client Name] at the time the referral fee is paid.

This referral fee is the responsibility of [Referree Name] and not [Client Name]. The referral fee will not increase the total amount of the fee charged to [Client Name].

By signing below, [Client Name], [Referrer Name], and [Referee Name] confirm that they understand and agree to the terms outlined above.

Date:

_____   _____
[Referrer Name]   **[Referree Name]**

_____
[Client Name]

The Referrer and Referree must maintain a completed copy of this Referral Agreement signed by the Referrer, Referree and the client in accordance with the Law Society's By-Law 9.

It is recommended that the client also keep a completed copy of this agreement for their files.

KEY TERMS

advertising, 56
business communication, 58
contingency fee, 68
fee splitting, 67
marketing, 57
referral agreement, 66
referral fee, 66
strategic planning, 58

USEFUL URLS

Canada Revenue Agency. 2017. "Penalties, Interest, and Other Consequences." <http://www.cra-arc.gc.ca/tx/bsnss/tpcs/pyrll/hwpyrllwrks/pnlty/menu-eng.html>.

Canada Revenue Agency Business Registration. <http://www.businessregistration.gc.ca>.

Human Rights Tribunal of Ontario. <http://www.sjto.gov.on.ca/HRTO/>.

Law Society of Upper Canada. 2017. "Frequently Asked Questions About Referral Fees." <http://www.lsuc.on.ca/with.aspx?id=2147503904&langtype=1033>.

Ministry of Labour. <http://www.labour.gov.on.ca>.

Ministry of Labour. 2017. "Employment Standards." <https://www.labour.gov.on.ca/english/es/index.php>.

Ontario Human Rights Commission. <http://www.ohrc.on.ca/en>.

REVIEW QUESTIONS

1. What is advertising?

2. What is marketing?

3. What is strategic planning?

4. What areas and issues does Rule 8 regulate?

5. What should paralegals consider when setting hourly fees/rates?

6. What do Rule 5.01(12) and Guideline 13 say about fee splitting?

7. Are paralegals permitted to charge clients contingency fees when those clients are facing criminal or quasi-criminal charges?

8. Is it permissible for a paralegal to enter into an oral agreement to represent a client without ever putting that agreement in writing?

9. What factors should paralegals consider when setting contingency fees?

10. What is "scooping"?

SCENARIO-BASED QUESTIONS

1. Legitimate Letterhead?

Pauline Lachance is opening a paralegal practice as a sole practitioner. She would like to make her firm look more impressive, so she is planning to add the words "and partners" after her name on her firm's letterhead. Is this permissible?

2. Cooperative Cousins

Jacinta Morelli, a licensed paralegal and a sole practitioner, would like to employ, as a paralegal, her newly licensed cousin Kyle Lambretta. She cannot afford to pay Kyle a salary, but would like him to share in a portion of the fees she bills clients. When Kyle brings a client to Jacinta, he will receive 70 percent of the fees billed, and when he works on a file for an existing client or a client secured by Jacinta, he will receive 25 percent of the fees billed. Does this arrangement breach the Rules? Why or why not?

3. Need a Hero?

Clark Kendall is a sole practitioner who has an idea for an ad that he would like to appear on billboards near his city's courthouse. Clark would be dressed in a blue cape with letters CK appearing in a black triangle on a blue t-shirt worn under the cape. The ad would say, "Stay out of the red by hiring me. If I don't win it's free!" Clark charges an administrative fee of $200 to open a file. That fee is not mentioned in the ad and is non-refundable. Is the wording of this ad permissible? What of the picture? Why or why not? Cite any relevant Rules and Guidelines.

4. Accidental Encounters

Wayne Randall was visiting his sister-in-law in the hospital. The other patient in the semi-private room, Lynda Frank, approached Wayne and said, "It's hard not to eavesdrop in here, but did you say you were a paralegal? I am here because I was in a car accident last week and I need someone to represent me. Could you come here tomorrow at 10 a.m. to discuss this?"

a. Wayne does not deal with statutory accident benefits claims, but he knows that one of his former classmates does. Wayne provides Lynda Frank with the contact information of his former classmate and sends his classmate an email saying, "I expect a 10% referral fee if you take her on." Is Wayne entitled to a referral fee in this circumstance? Explain your answer citing the relevant Rules and Guidelines.

b. Clive Warren regularly hangs around in hospitals trying to sign up clients. He has visited Lynda Frank three times, pressing her to retain him, and becomes extremely angry when he overhears Wayne providing Lynda with his classmate's contact information. Clive shouts, "Stop scooping my client!" Has Wayne "scooped" Lynda Frank? Explain your answer.

c. Does Clive's conduct violate any Rules and/or Guidelines?

5. Jamie's Job?

Jamie Waters is being interviewed by Simone Lewis, a licensed paralegal. The position Jamie is applying for is that of file clerk. At the beginning of the interview Simone looks at Jamie and says: "Jamie is a gender-neutral name. I'm sorry, but I can't tell, are you male or female?" When she asked this question, did Simone Lewis violate the *Human Rights Code*? Explain your answer.

Clients and the Public

6

LEARNING OUTCOMES

After completing this chapter, you should be able to:

- Understand the obligations of paralegals with respect to competence.

- Understand the obligations of paralegals with respect to client identification and verification.

- Understand the obligations of paralegals with respect to advising clients.

- Understand the obligations of paralegals with respect to confidentiality.

- Identify who "clients" are and understand the duties of paralegals to their clients.

- Understand the obligations of paralegals with respect to conflicts of interest.

- Understand how to use technology effectively, in accordance with the Rules and your professional obligations, in your communications with clients.

- Recognize the requirement in Rule 8.04 and part II of By-Law 6 for errors and omissions insurance, and understand its importance.

- Understand best practices for, and know how to create, a retainer agreement.

- Understand best practices for, and know how to create, a non-engagement letter.

Dealing with Clients

client
a person who (a) consults a paralegal and on whose behalf the paralegal provides or agrees to provide legal services, or (b) having consulted the paralegal, reasonably concludes that the paralegal has agreed to act on his or her behalf; includes a client of the firm of which the paralegal is a partner or associate, whether or not the paralegal handles the client's work (Rule 1.02)

competent paralegal
a paralegal who has and applies the relevant skills, attributes, and values appropriate to each matter undertaken on a client's behalf (Rule 3.01(4))

Unlike customers, who purchase products, **clients** are purchasers of services—for example, legal services. Rule 3 of the LSUC's *Paralegal Rules of Conduct*[1] sets out the duties of paralegals to their clients. You must balance these duties with your duties to the administration of justice and the general public.

Competence

According to Rule 3.01(1), paralegals must perform all services undertaken on a client's behalf to the standard of a competent paralegal. A **competent paralegal** is a paralegal who has and applies the relevant skills, attributes, and values appropriate to each matter undertaken on a client's behalf (Rule 3.01(4)). These may include—but are not limited to—legal research, analysis, writing and drafting, negotiation, and advocacy.

As Guideline 6 of the LSUC's *Paralegal Professional Conduct Guidelines*[2] points out, clients who hire paralegals have the expectation that those paralegals are competent and have the ability to properly represent them. Section 2 of that guideline provides that paralegals "should not undertake a matter without honestly feeling competent to handle it, or being able to become competent without undue delay, risk, or expense to the client."

In addition, section 4 of that guideline indicates that competence involves "more than an understanding of legal principles; it involves an adequate knowledge of the practice and procedures by which such principles can be effectively applied." It is also a requirement that paralegals be aware of developments in all areas of law in which they practise.

> In *Law Society of Upper Canada v McLean*, 2014 ONLSTH 100, the agreed statement of facts indicated that the paralegal was retained to represent a client charged with a traffic offence, and negotiated a deal with the prosecutor that resulted in the client being convicted of a charge that carried a greater number of demerit points than that attached to the original offence. The paralegal did not consult the relevant legislation to determine the demerit points applicable to the offence and he did not obtain the client's instructions before entering into the agreement. The unhappy client appealed the conviction, using a different paralegal to do so, and, in the course of that proceeding, the judge made an order compelling the paralegal to appear. The paralegal failed to do so. Although subsequently issued a bench summons and ordered to attend court with his client file, the paralegal advised the prosecutor that he had a scheduling conflict and did not attend. This clear instance of a lack of competence (in addition to a failure to secure instructions) resulted in the imposition of a $2,000 fine and $2,000 in costs payable to the LSUC.

---

1   Law Society of Upper Canada, *Paralegal Rules of Conduct* (1 October 2014; amendments current to 2017), online: <https://www.lsuc.on.ca/paralegal-conduct-rules>.

2   Law Society of Upper Canada, *Paralegal Professional Conduct Guidelines* (1 October 2014; amendments current to 2016), online: <http://www.lsuc.on.ca/paralegal-conduct-guidelines>.

Directly related to this requirement, the LSUC's mandated continuing professional development (By-Law 6.1)[3] requires practising paralegals to complete at least 12 hours in eligible education activities per year, including 3 hours (known as **Professionalism Hours**) "on topics related to professional responsibility, ethics and/or practice management and up to 9 **Substantive Hours** per year."[4] Professionalism Hours must be accredited by the LSUC. Substantive Hours generally deal with developments in various areas of law, particular skills, and/or practice and procedure. Substantive Hours need not be accredited by the LSUC. Although this may not be enough to ensure competence in particular areas of law, it is a minimum requirement and paralegals are encouraged to do more than the minimum in order to fulfill their professional obligations to their clients. Rule 3.01(4)(j) and (k) refer to the paralegal's obligation of "pursuing appropriate training and development to maintain and enhance knowledge and skills" and indicate that competence includes the ability to adapt "to changing requirements, standards, techniques and practices."

Section 15 of Guideline 6 explicitly states: "A paralegal is responsible for remaining competent throughout his or her career. A competent paralegal understands that maintaining competence is an ongoing professional commitment that requires the paralegal to constantly assess his or her knowledge and skills."

Rule 3.01(4)(l) states that paralegals must comply with the Rules "in letter and in spirit"—in other words, as a professional you are expected to embrace the Rules to the fullest extent. It is not appropriate to look for loopholes or gaps to exploit.

To be competent, you must be able to properly perform any task that you agree to take on. Part of this involves recognizing the limitations of your training and expertise. You must not attempt to perform tasks that are too complex for you to properly complete or undertake to do things you cannot handle. If you discover in the course of a matter that you do not possess the knowledge or experience necessary for you to continue, you should obtain the client's consent to consult with a lawyer, or refer the file to another paralegal. It is not worth risking your reputation and licence by working on matters that are outside your area or areas of expertise when there are other matters that you can competently manage on your own.

Professionalism Hours
hours of continuing professional development covering topics such as ethics, professional responsibility, and/or practice management

Substantive Hours
hours of continuing professional development that generally deal with topics such as developments in various areas of law, particular skills, and/or practice and procedure

Advising Clients

Rule 3.02 requires paralegals to be honest and candid when advising clients, and to provide advice only within their permitted scope of practice. For example, paralegals should not provide financial advice, since they are not licensed to do so.

Section 5 of Guideline 6 states, "The competent paralegal will ensure that only after all necessary information has been gathered, reviewed and considered does he or she advise the client as to the course(s) of action that will most likely meet the client's goals, taking care to ensure that the client is made aware of all foreseeable risks and/or costs associated with the course(s) of action." Thus, it is important to give careful consideration to a client's matter before providing advice to that client.

---

3   Law Society of Upper Canada, By-Law 6.1 (29 January 2009; repealed and replaced 25 September 2013, effective 1 January 2014), online: <https://www.lsuc.on.ca/by-laws/>.

4   Law Society of Upper Canada, "Continuing Professional Development Requirement," online: <https://www.lsuc.on.ca/CPD-Requirement/>.

The advice that paralegals may give to clients is also limited by their broader duties to the public and to the administration of justice. You may not knowingly assist in or encourage any dishonesty, fraud, crime, or illegal conduct—for example, you may not advise a client to lie under oath or in a sworn affidavit, or how to break the law and avoid punishment (Rule 3.02(4)).

Paralegals must take reasonable measures to avoid becoming the "tool or dupe"(this is the language used in prior versions of the Rules) of an unscrupulous client or that client's associates (Rule 3.02(4)). Interestingly, the disciplinary decisions dealing with situations in which a licensee was found to be a "tool or dupe" of an unscrupulous client tend to involve lawyers who were involved in real estate transactions and, often, mortgage fraud. Although paralegals are not permitted to practise real estate law, it is certainly possible that they too will be found to have been used by clients to "facilitate dishonesty, fraud, crime or illegal conduct," in violation of Rule 3.02(7) and section 27 of By-Law 7.1.

Paralegals should not accept large cash retainers and return the funds by cheque; this is a common form of money laundering. From a practice management perspective, you must be careful about the clients you take on, and you must scrutinize the instructions you are given to satisfy yourself that you are not being used for illegal purposes. Guideline 7, section 6 warns paralegals that "[a] client or another person may attempt to use a paralegal's trust account for improper purposes, such as hiding funds, money laundering or tax sheltering. These situations highlight the fact that when handling trust funds, it is important for a paralegal to be aware of his or her obligations under the Rules and the Law Society's By-Laws regulating the handling of trust funds."

Where the client is an organization, Rule 3.02(8) imposes additional responsibilities upon the paralegal. The paralegal is to advise the person from whom he or she takes instructions and/or the chief legal officer "that the organization has acted, is acting or intends to act dishonestly, fraudulently, criminally, or illegally" and that the conduct should be stopped; if the conduct does not cease, the paralegal is to continue up the chain of command, providing the same information and advice. If the organization continues to engage in the wrongful conduct, the paralegal is obliged to withdraw from acting in the matter. More information on withdrawing from representation is provided under the heading "Withdrawal from Representation," later in this chapter.

Rule 3.02(11) obligates paralegals to encourage their clients to compromise or settle a dispute whenever doing so is possible on a reasonable basis. Guideline 7, section 10 states:

> … the paralegal should seek the client's instructions to make an offer of settlement to the other party as soon as reasonably possible. As soon as possible after receipt of an offer of settlement from the other party, the paralegal must explain to the client the terms of the offer, the implications of accepting the offer and the possibility of making a counter-offer. When making an offer of settlement, a paralegal should allow the other party reasonable time for review and acceptance of the offer. The paralegal should not make, accept or reject an offer of settlement without the client's clear and informed instructions. To avoid any misunderstandings, the paralegal should confirm the client's instructions in writing.

You must also inform your clients about alternative dispute resolution options—such as mediation, negotiation, or arbitration—and advise them regarding the availability and feasibility of each of these (Rule 3.02(12)).

Paralegals should never add fuel to the fire of a conflict for their own purposes—namely, to create more fees. While resolving matters quickly may mean that you make less money on each file, a paralegal business is not only a business for the purpose of maximizing earnings, but a profession with the numerous responsibilities and obligations imposed by the LSUC.

When dealing with clients with a disability (Rules 3.02(13) and (14))—that is, clients whose ability to make decisions is impaired because of age, mental disability, or for some other reason—paralegals should maintain a normal professional relationship with such clients as far as is reasonably possible. However, if a client loses the capacity to manage his or her legal affairs, you must take steps to have a representative appointed for that client.

Guideline 6, section 3.1 and Guideline 7, section 12 address persons with diminished capacity and limited scope retainers. It provides that the paralegal should carefully consider and assess in each case if, under the circumstances, it is possible to render those services in a competent manner and in compliance with Rules 3.02(13) and (14).

See also Guideline 7, section 11, which advises the paralegal to be particularly sensitive to the individual needs of clients with disabilities and to be aware of the duty to accommodate clients with disabilities.

For French-speaking clients, paralegals must advise them of their official language rights, including their right to be served by a paralegal who speaks French (Rule 3.02(22); Guideline 7, section 16). If you take on a client who chooses to be served in French, then you must be competent to serve the client in that language (Rule 3.02(23)). You should consider networking with paralegals who provide services in French so that you can refer clients as necessary.

Confidentiality

Like certain other professionals, such as physicians and social workers, paralegals have a duty to keep client matters confidential, as outlined in Rule 3.03 and Guideline 8. Notably, however, paralegals do not generally fall within the more stringent protections offered lawyers under the rules of solicitor–client privilege. Even so, clients are entitled to trust that paralegals will hold their confidential information in strict confidence. **Confidential information** is any information that paralegals gain in the course of their professional relationship with a client. To ensure confidentiality, paralegals must keep the client's papers and other property out of the sight and reach of those who are not entitled to see them.

The duty of confidentiality continues indefinitely after the paralegal has finished acting for a client. However, paralegals may be required to disclose confidential information in certain situations—for example, when required by law or order of a tribunal (Rule 3.03(4)). Paralegals may disclose confidential information to defend against allegations of criminal wrongdoing, malpractice, or misconduct (Rule 3.03(6)). In addition, paralegals may disclose what confidential information is necessary to collection agencies attempting to collect unpaid accounts on behalf of those paralegals (Rule 3.03(7); Guideline 8, section 16). A paralegal seeking to obtain legal advice about his

confidential information any information that paralegals gain in the course of their professional relationship with a client; paralegals have a duty to hold all such information in strict confidence indefinitely and may not disclose it to any other person, unless authorized to do so by the client or required to do so by law (Rule 3.03(1))

or her proposed conduct may also disclose confidential information to a lawyer or paralegal in order to do so (Rule 3.03(8)). In all cases, the paralegal may only disclose confidential information that is necessary for the particular purpose (Rule 3.03(9)).

Confidentiality, like advising clients, is an area where your duties to your client and your duties to the general public and the administration of justice may conflict. Under Rule 3.03(5), paralegals may disclose confidential information relating to a client if they have reasonable grounds to believe that there is an imminent risk of death or serious bodily harm—including serious psychological harm that substantially interferes with health or well-being—to an identifiable person or group, and that disclosing the confidential information is necessary to prevent the death or harm. For example, if a client tells you that he will kill his landlord with the gun he bought last week if the broken furnace is not fixed and you reasonably believe that he may carry through on this threat, you *may* disclose the threat to the police, though you are not obligated to. Guideline 8, sections 13 and 14 interpret this rule, and section 14 also indicates that paralegals would do well to consider a number of factors, including the apparent absence of any other feasible way to prevent the potential injury and the circumstances under which the information was acquired from the client. Section 15 of that same guideline indicates that if confidential information is disclosed, the paralegal should "record the circumstances of the disclosure as soon as possible." It is very important to keep a detailed written record of the events surrounding the disclosure and the nature of the information disclosed.

Although conflicts of interest are discussed in more detail later in this chapter under the heading "Conflicts of Interest and Identifying Clients," it is interesting to note that Rule 3.03(10) provides that paralegals may also disclose confidential information as necessary to detect and resolve conflicts of interest arising from their change of employment or changes in the composition or ownership of a paralegal firm. The information disclosed must not compromise client confidentiality or otherwise prejudice the client. Guideline 8, sections 16.1 through 16.4 indicate that the information disclosed should be limited to the names of the persons involved in a matter, a brief summary of the general issues involved, and information as to whether the representation has ended. In addition, the guideline indicates that ideally disclosure should be limited to one person, but, at any rate, to as few people at the new firm as possible. Furthermore, the information is to be securely stored, returned, or destroyed in a confidential matter as appropriate. Section 16.5 of Guideline 8 indicates that the client's consent may be addressed in a retainer agreement, although in some circumstances the paralegal who transfers to a new firm may be required to obtain the client's consent to that disclosure. Again, the key consideration is the potential prejudice to the client in disclosing the information. In that context, the example cited in that guideline is that of a client who consulted with a paralegal about a criminal investigation that has not led to a public charge.

In addition, the client may authorize the disclosure of confidential information by the paralegal, in which case Guideline 8, sections 9 and 10 are relevant. The paralegal must ensure that the client understands both the right to confidentiality and the implications of waiving that right. In general, it is advisable to secure the client's written authorization to disclose confidential information. Review "Planning for Practice: Confidentially Speaking," below, and consider the issues raised by Amanda Watson's discussion with her employee.

PLANNING FOR PRACTICE

Confidentially Speaking

Since becoming a licensed paralegal five years ago, Amanda Watson has worked on many challenging summary conviction criminal cases. She has built quite a reputation for mastering details and taking a tough stance when defending her clients.

None have been more challenging than her current case.

Her client, a local TV personality, has been charged with impaired driving and failing to stop at the scene of an accident. He had been out for dinner with a colleague one night and while returning home he rear-ended an SUV stopped at a red light. The TV personality fled the scene and was arrested two hours later at his home. No one was injured in the collision.

The case has drawn significant interest in the local media and plenty of people in the community are talking about it in bars and coffee shops.

With the much-anticipated trial scheduled to begin Monday morning at 9:30 a.m., Amanda and her legal assistant Toni worked long hours the week before, preparing every detail of the case, preparing witnesses, and reviewing every piece of the Crown's disclosure.

The Friday afternoon before the trial, Amanda and Toni decided to take a break from preparations to have lunch at a popular trendy restaurant just around the corner of the office. They were seated at a small table tucked away near the back of the restaurant where they could have a more private conversation.

The lunch conversation started simply enough. Amanda was curious to know all about Toni's plans for her upcoming vacation to Spain once the trial was over. Amanda was reminiscing about her own experiences in Madrid and Barcelona, and was keen to make recommendations for things to do, since this would be Toni's first time there.

Not long after the appetizers were cleared and their glasses of wine were topped up, the conversation turned to work. It started with them discussing their frustrations with one particularly difficult client who was consistently being uncooperative in preparing for his case. It wasn't long before they began talking about their current high-profile case.

That conversation mainly focused on how nervous Amanda was about trying the case with all the extra attention it was generating. The trial was scheduled for two days and not only would she have to try the case, but she would have to manage the extra expectations of dealing with the media and answering questions.

At another point in the conversation, Amanda leaned in closer and lowered her voice. She told Toni how apprehensive she was about how one key witness would perform on the stand. The witness, a bartender at the restaurant where her client had had dinner the night of the incident, would be testifying how many drinks he had served him. Amanda wasn't so sure how he would hold up on cross-examination.

Toni was quick to reassure Amanda that she had a strong case, that they were well prepared, and that she would handle herself brilliantly in court.

Even though they hadn't gone to lunch intending to discuss work, Amanda felt more at ease and the two returned to the office to continue their preparations.

Was this conversation appropriate to have over lunch? Try to identify all the ways in which Amanda and Toni may have breached confidentiality or behaved inappropriately. How might they have handled matters differently?

You should note that a paralegal's professional obligation of confidentiality is distinct from the legal doctrine of solicitor–client privilege, whereby certain communications between a lawyer and a client are legally protected from disclosure and are inadmissible in court. This is a broader protection than confidentiality, since a court may order confidential communications to be disclosed in certain circumstances. Although the doctrine of privilege generally does not apply to communications between a paralegal and a client, there is case law in which certain communications made by a client to a paralegal were held to be privileged (see, for example, *R v McClure*).[5]

Conflicts of Interest and Identifying Clients

conflict of interest
the existence of a substantial risk that a paralegal's loyalty to or representation of a client would be materially and adversely affected by the paralegal's own interest or the paralegal's duties to another client, a former client, or a third person; the risk must be more than a mere possibility; there must be a genuine, serious risk to the duty of loyalty or to client representation arising from the retainer

Paralegals are obligated to act with loyalty to their clients. This means that they must represent the interests of each client exclusively. There are numerous circumstances that may present a **conflict of interest**, defined in Rule 1.02 as the existence of a substantial risk that a paralegal's loyalty to or representation of a client would be materially and adversely affected by the paralegal's own interest or the paralegal's duties to another client, a former client, or a third person. The risk must be more than a mere possibility; there must be a genuine, serious risk to the duty of loyalty or to client representation arising from the **retainer**. The interest may be a financial interest, but it may be an interest of a different nature. For example, it would be a conflict of interest to act as paralegal to your landlord in drafting a tenancy agreement because your personal interests might conflict with those of your client. Similarly, it might be a conflict of interest to act for a client who is suing your cousin in Small Claims Court. You must avoid conflicts of interest in your dealings with clients. Where this is not possible, you should refer clients to another paralegal or lawyer.

retainer
the advance payment made by a client, usually at the time that the retainer agreement is signed, that is deposited in the paralegal's trust account

A conflict of interest will arise if your loyalty and ability to represent a client's interests are compromised, or even if these *appear* to be compromised. Rules 3.04, 3.05, and 3.06 provide that a paralegal may not

transaction with a client
a transaction to which a paralegal and a client of the paralegal are parties, whether or not other persons are also parties; includes lending or borrowing money, buying or selling property or services having other than nominal value, giving or acquiring ownership, security, or other pecuniary interest in a company or other entity, recommending an investment, or entering into a common business venture

- act against former clients in the same matter or any related matter, unless the former client consents;
- act against persons involved or associated with a former client in a matter, unless the client's written consent is obtained;
- represent more than one side in a dispute;
- represent a client in a matter where there is a conflict of interest between that client and another client unless there is express or implied consent from all clients and it is reasonable for the paralegal to conclude that he or she is able to represent those clients without having a "material adverse effect upon the representation of or loyalty to the other client";
- enter into a **transaction with a client** unless the transaction is fair and reasonable to the client; or
- borrow from a client (except from a regulated lender or related person).

---

5   2001 SCC 14, [2001] 1 SCR 445.

In a 2015 decision of the Ontario Superior Court of Justice, *Trillium Motor World Ltd v General Motors of Canada Ltd*, 2015 ONSC 3824, the court awarded the sum of $45,000,000 in aggregated damages to the plaintiffs in a class action lawsuit against the law firm Cassels Brock & Blackwell LLP. The court held that the law firm had breached its fiduciary duties by accepting the retainer by General Motors of Canada Limited dealers when it had already agreed to act for the federal government in relation to those proceedings. The court held that the law firm had known of the conflict from the outset, but failed to decline to act for the dealers or to tell the dealers about its retainer by the federal government. In addition, the court held that there was a conflict in the interests of different categories of dealers: those which had signed agreements to terminate their relationships with General Motors of Canada Limited and those which had not done so, yet the firm continued to represent both categories of dealers. This decision is under appeal.

As mentioned above, the term "client" has an expansive meaning under the Rules. It includes, but is not limited to, a client of the paralegal firm of which the paralegal is a partner or employee, whether or not the paralegal handles the client's work (Rule 1.02). In other words, your partner's clients are your clients, and vice versa. This is an important concept to keep in mind when you are considering conflicts of interest. If your partner or employee is representing a party to a dispute, you may not represent the opposing party, as this would be a conflict of interest. For the purpose of assessing whether there is a conflict of interest, former clients of your firm are considered clients.

A common question that arises in various situations is: Who is the client? Although it may seem obvious that the client is the person with whom the paralegal (or firm) contracts to provide legal services, identifying who the client is can be difficult. To comply with Rule 3, it is imperative that you make clear to all involved in a matter who is and who is not a client, particularly in cases where one party to a dispute is unrepresented. Consider the following:

1. An officer, director, or shareholder of a corporation comes into your office. Who will you be representing—the individual or the corporation?

Where there is a corporation involved, you should clarify the client's identity at your initial meeting. You may represent either the corporation or an individual, such as a shareholder or director, but probably not both. For example, if there is more than one shareholder, the interests of the corporation are not necessarily aligned with the interests of any particular shareholder.

2. You are paid by the parent of a young person charged with a minor criminal offence. Whose instructions do you follow?

If you are paid by someone other than the client, make sure that the client is aware of the payment arrangement and consents to it. Ensure that everyone understands that you are representing the client, not the payer—and that you take instructions from the client only.

3. You are representing a landlord in a landlord–tenant matter in which the tenant is unrepresented. In the process of negotiating on behalf of your client, the tenant asks you questions about the law. What do you say?

If you are negotiating with an unrepresented party, that party must be aware that you are not acting as a mediator or providing assistance to both your client and that party, but you are representing only your client. You should encourage the unrepresented party to seek **independent legal advice**.

4. You are representing two co-accused who tell the same story. Later, one co-accused points the finger at the other. What do you do?

Often in the course of legal matters, the interests of two or more clients that initially appeared to coincide begin to conflict. In this case, you may not be able to represent either client because the confidential information you have gathered creates a conflict of interest.

---

independent legal advice/independent legal representation
legal advice provided by a legal representative to represent the interests of a person or organization who requires legal service from a different legal services provider because of a conflict of interest that prevents the paralegal who was originally consulted from giving advice to the person or organization

---

Conflicts of interest may also develop as a result of the paralegal's personal relationship, that is, when representing friends or family members. The Rules permit paralegals to represent those persons, but Guideline 9, section 47 requires the paralegal to consider several factors before accepting the retainer, including the following:

- the client's vulnerability (emotional and financial);
- the possibility that a power imbalance will be created;
- whether the personal relationship may jeopardize the client's right to confidentiality;
- whether the paralegal may be required to act as a witness in the matter; and
- whether the relationship may interfere with the paralegal's fiduciary obligations to the client.

If the paralegal is not a sole practitioner, it would be advisable for him or her to refer the potential client to another paralegal or lawyer at the firm who does not have a personal relationship with that client (Guideline 9, section 48).

Paralegals have specific obligations concerning client identification and verification as mandated in By-Law 7.1, part III. When a paralegal is retained to provide legal services or engages in or gives instructions about receiving, paying, or transferring funds, he or she must obtain detailed information about the client and take steps to verify the client's identity. Where the client is an individual, that information includes

- full name;
- home address and home telephone number;
- business address and phone number (if applicable); and
- occupation(s).

If the client is an organization, other than a financial institution, public body, or reporting issuer, the identification requirements include

- the organization's incorporation or business identification number and the place of issue of that organization or business identification number (if applicable); and
- the name, position, and contact information for each individual who gives instructions with respect to the matter for which the paralegal is retained.

For organizations other than securities dealers, the paralegal is also to make reasonable efforts to ascertain

- the name and occupation or occupations of each director of the organization; and
- the name, address, and occupation or occupations of each person who owns 25 percent or more of the organization or shares in that organization.

The by-law specifies that, in the case of organizations, the licensee must verify the identity of the organization no later than 60 days after engaging in or giving instructions in respect of the receiving, paying, or transferring of funds.

The by-law lists a number of independent source documents, such as driver's licences, that can be used to verify an individual client's identity. Where the client is incorporated, a certificate of corporate status issued by a public body is used to verify the client's identity. For corporations incorporated in Ontario, the certificate is issued by the Ministry of Government and Consumer Services, while for federally incorporated corporations, the certificate is issued by Corporations Canada. The identification and verification obligations also apply to clients whom the paralegal has not met in person. Special considerations apply to paralegals who are required to identify and verify the identities of clients not present in Canada.

Phantom Clients

A **phantom client** is someone who believes that he or she is represented by a paralegal even though he or she has not formally retained or hired that paralegal (Guideline 5, section 8). Phantom clients create problems for the paralegal because he or she may owe duties to these persons, but may not realize this because he or she has not identified the person as a client. Section 10 of Guideline 5 recommends that paralegals "avoid discussing legal matters outside the working environment or a working relationship." What a paralegal views as a social conversation may give the person discussing his or her legal matter with the paralegal the impression that the paralegal is now acting for that person. According to Guideline 5, section 9, "One of the common ways in which phantom clients are created is through a person who consults with the paralegal on a matter but does not clearly indicate whether he or she wants to hire the paralegal or pursue the matter."

Paralegals should be careful to avoid creating the impression that they represent someone until they are formally retained. If a paralegal believes that the person who has consulted him or her may be confused about the role of the paralegal and

phantom client
someone who believes that he or she is represented by a paralegal even though he or she has not formally retained or hired that paralegal

retainer letter
a letter from the paralegal
or paralegal firm to the
client; the letter confirms
the existence of a retainer,
the scope of that retainer,
and generally contains
the same information as a
retainer agreement, but is
not signed by the client

retainer agreement
a contract between two
parties through which
one pays to reserve the
time of the other and
secures the performance
of professional services

non-engagement letter
a letter from the paralegal
or paralegal firm to someone who has consulted that
paralegal or paralegal firm
that clearly indicates that
the paralegal or paralegal
firm has not been retained
in the matter that was the
subject of the consultation

whether the paralegal has been retained, the paralegal should confirm his or her understanding of his or her role by preparing a retainer letter, a retainer agreement, or a non-engagement letter. A **retainer letter** is a letter from the paralegal or paralegal firm to the client. The letter confirms the existence of a retainer and the scope of that retainer, and generally contains the same information as a retainer agreement, but unlike the retainer agreement, it is not signed by the client. A **retainer agreement** is a contract between two parties through which one pays to reserve the time of the other and secures the performance of professional services (see the heading "Retainer Agreements" in this chapter for a discussion of the content of those agreements). A **non-engagement letter** is a letter from the paralegal or paralegal firm to someone who has consulted that paralegal or paralegal firm that clearly indicates that the paralegal or paralegal firm has not been retained in the matter that was the subject of the consultation.

Non-engagement letters should specifically refer to any limitation periods in the matter that was the subject of the consultation. If the limitation is clearly set out in the non-engagement letter, this gives the recipient of the letter a clear indication both that the paralegal is not accepting the case and that a limitation period applies to the case. This serves as a prompt to the recipient to secure representation prior to the expiration of that limitation period. The consequences of missing a limitation period should be explained in the letter. If a limitation period is about to expire, the letter is to refer the recipient to the relevant statute and advise him or her that it is urgent for him or her to take prompt action. Actions brought outside limitation periods are statute-barred, and missed limitation periods can result in complaints to the LSUC as well as negligence claims against paralegals.

The non-engagement letter should clearly indicate the date of the consultation and should explain why the paralegal will not represent the individual (this may be due to a conflict of interest, as discussed in this chapter under the heading "Conflicts of Interest and Identifying Clients"). When the retainer is declined due to a conflict of interest, the non-engagement letter should confirm that you have recommended that the recipient secure independent legal representation. Securing independent legal representation, also referred to as obtaining independent legal advice, is simply securing a legal representative to represent the interests of a person or organization who requires legal advice. The word "independent" is used because often there is a conflict of interest that prevents a paralegal from giving advice to the person or organization so that person or organization must consult a different legal services provider.

A non-engagement letter should not express a legal opinion concerning the merits of the matter unless the paralegal has conducted the legal research necessary to reach that conclusion. If, at the consultation, the individual or members of the organization provided documents or other property to the paralegal during the consultation, then the return of those documents and that property is to be effected with the delivery of the non-engagement letter, and the letter is to explicitly confirm the return of that material. The non-engagement letter should be kept in a file containing non-engagement letters or a client file, and information relating to the consultation should be included in the conflicts checking system.

For a sample non-engagement letter, see Appendix 6.1 to this chapter.

Withdrawal from Representation

Rule 3.08 and Guideline 11 govern withdrawal from representation, including circumstances where this is optional, mandatory, and prohibited. Unlike other professionals, who may "fire" their clients at will, paralegals may not withdraw their services whenever they wish—particularly when representing clients in criminal and quasi-criminal matters. This is because of the significant consequences that may result for their clients, who may not be able to retain new counsel in time to meet deadlines or attend court dates.

Even if a client refuses or is unable to pay you, once you have been retained there are limits on your ability to withdraw. You may be required to go to court to show that your client's case will not be prejudiced if you withdraw from representation. If no prejudice to your client will result, you may withdraw in the circumstances set out in Rule 3.08. Generally, you may withdraw if you have lost confidence in your client's ability to inform you of the facts in a forthright and honest manner, or if your client has lost confidence in you for any reason. You may also usually withdraw if your client is failing to pay your fees. You must provide notice of your intention to withdraw, and provide the client with a reasonable opportunity to pay. You may not use the threat of withdrawal to push your client to make a difficult decision—for example, to settle. However, if the client deceives you or refuses to accept and act upon your advice on a significant point, you may withdraw from representation (Rule 3.08(3); Guideline 11, section 10). Review "Planning for Practice: Withdrawal from Representation," below, and consider what actions you would take if you were the paralegal representing this client.

PLANNING FOR PRACTICE

Withdrawal from Representation

Zack Hrenyk was arrested for impaired driving after police pulled him over while driving home from a Saturday night of drinking with his buddies at a local pub. He was released from custody and ordered to return to the police station Monday morning for booking and fingerprinting.

A week later, after he made his first court appearance, Zack sought legal representation. He intended to challenge the police allegation that he was at nearly double the legal limit at the time of his arrest, citing a faulty roadside screening device that he noticed the officer was having difficulty operating.

Zack met with Andrew Redden, a licensed paralegal who used to work for one of the best-known criminal defence firms in the city and had recently started his own practice. After reviewing the Crown's disclosure and arrest documents, Andrew determined Zack could mount a credible defence, and agreed to take on the case.

Andrew immediately requested additional disclosure from the Crown, including breathalyzer calibration reports, in-car video, and officer training records. The Crown was slow to provide these records, which resulted in the court adjourning the case twice.

Zack arrived 20 minutes late for the next court appearance, leaving Andrew to request that the case be held until he arrived. Adding further insult, Zack had a faint smell of alcohol on his breath. The case was called again and the judge remarked "nice of you to show up, Mr. Hrenyk."

Zack pleaded not guilty to the charge and a court date to set the matter for trial was scheduled for six weeks later.

Although he was not required to attend that appearance, Zack showed up nearly half an hour after the court session had begun. The case was called, and Andrew, the Crown, and the presiding judge agreed to set trial for June 11 at 10 a.m.

Zack stood up and, in a somewhat loud and disruptive voice, told the judge that the date did not work for him.

"I'm going to Cuba that week," he said. "I won't be here."

Andrew sought a brief adjournment to speak with his client. He sternly told Zack that the court does not work around his vacation schedule. He also advised Zack that rescheduling would push the case to the fall and draw the ire of the judge.

Zack agreed to change his vacation plans and the June date was set.

Two weeks before the trial, Andrew called Zack to schedule a trial preparation session. Zack showed up late for that session and seemed generally disinterested.

"Why do I need to go through this?" he asked. "You're supposed to fight this."

The day of the trial, Zack failed to show up 30 minutes early as planned. Andrew called and Zack explained he was on the beach in Cuba. "I though you knew that," he said.

This was the final straw.

Andrew informed the court that Zack defied instructions and went on holiday. Andrew also told the court and the Crown present that he no longer had confidence in his client and wished to withdraw from representing Zack in this case.

Because the trial would likely be adjourned until September, leaving little time for another paralegal to be retained and to adequately prepare for trial, Andrew knew he would need the court's approval to "fire" Zack.

The judge agreed to adjourn the case and hold a hearing on Andrew's request to withdraw from the case two weeks later. At that hearing Andrew's request was granted.

Do you think Andrew was right to withdraw from the case or should he have stuck with it to ensure Zack's trial rights were preserved?

Rule 3.08 requires you to withdraw if your client is demanding that you conduct yourself in violation of the Rules, or By-Laws, as mentioned earlier in the chapter, or if you are not competent to handle the matter. Withdrawal from representation is also mandatory if your client terminates the paralegal–client relationship. In addition, Guideline 7, section 4 provides that paralegals may need to withdraw from representing clients who engage in dishonesty or illegal conduct.

Section 24(b) of By-Law 7.1 also mandates withdrawal from representation in cases in which the paralegal, while in the process of complying with client identification or verification requirements of that by-law, knows or ought to know that he or she is or would be assisting a client in fraud or other illegal conduct.

Technology and Client Communications

Advances in communications technology have revolutionized the way in which legal services are provided today. Legal research, administration, the drafting of documents, and even filings can now be done electronically, and communications with clients are often carried out online. Regardless of whether you are communicating by paper, by email, over the telephone, or in person, you are held to the same standards of professionalism and competence outlined in Rules 2 and 3. Adopting an informal tone in email, "blogging" about confidential client information, or discussing confidential matters in social networking forums are all examples of ways that paralegals might breach their professional obligations through misuse of technology. You should be as formal in your electronic communications as you are when using more traditional forms of written communication, and should retain copies of all electronic communications with clients.

You are responsible for ensuring the confidentiality of client information in electronic form. To this end, you may need to use firewalls, antivirus software, and passwords to ensure that third parties cannot access client information. You should also include a statement on emails indicating that they are intended to be confidential. Posting confidential client information online, whether on purpose or inadvertently, can give rise to complaints against you to the LSUC, and to lawsuits for negligence and defamation.

The following suggestions will help you foster solid client relationships, and will allow you and your clients to derive the greatest benefit from your use of technology:

- Personalize your voice mail: Clients telephone offices to speak with a person and will be unhappy to receive an automated response. If voice mail is necessary, you should frequently re-record your outgoing message with date and time statements, and should include a commitment to return calls within a certain timeframe.

- Set up systems mindfully: Position computers, faxes, and other communications technologies in such a way as to ensure ease of access and protect confidentiality. Make sure that systems are properly maintained, and employ or contract out appropriate technical support services. Ensure that your software systems are secure, and that they are shielded from viruses and security breaches. Do not share email or other identifying information about clients without their consent.

- Be reachable and communicate sensibly: Technology should make your life easier, and should make it easier for your clients to communicate with you. Clients should be able to access your direct voice mail or email quickly, and you should pick up or read messages promptly to determine their urgency. Clients should only be sent relevant communications. If you spam your clients with irrelevant information, they are more likely to miss important communications when you do send these. Remember that Rule 2 requires you to act with courtesy and civility, and prohibits all forms of harassment.

- Draw the line: Communication technologies allow us to work at any time, from almost anywhere. However, just because we *can* respond to client communications instantly does not mean that we should. A considered response sent after an appropriate time period will serve the client's interests and help you maintain a healthy work schedule.

For more information regarding the use of technology in your practice, consult the technology section of the LSUC's *Practice Management Guidelines*.[6]

Retainer Agreements

As stated earlier in the chapter, a retainer agreement is a contract between two parties through which one pays to reserve the time of the other and secures the performance of professional services. Where the retainer is for legal services, the paralegal or lawyer who is retained is obligated to act for the client. Consequently, he or she is prevented from acting for another party in the same dispute without the client's consent or for an opposing party in another matter at a later date.

From a practice management perspective, a retainer agreement serves several important functions:

- It is a tool for explaining and clarifying the paralegal's professional obligations. You may wish to inform your client, for example, that court procedures may be delayed due to factors beyond your control. Clearly define who your client is, and outline the scope of the retainer—what services you will and will not provide. This will reduce the risk of misunderstanding.

- It is a method for managing client expectations. Being upfront and transparent about the cost of legal fees reduces the likelihood of disputes regarding bills and increases the likelihood that you will collect fees for the services you provide. For example, you may wish to inform your client in the agreement that he or she will be charged for all telephone calls, emails, and messages.

- It can provide a defence in the event of a lawsuit or a complaint. If the details of the retainer agreement are explicit, fair, and clear, this may protect you from potential lawsuits by the client and/or complaints to the LSUC should a misunderstanding on any of the issues described above arise.

A retainer agreement should be made in writing at the beginning of the paralegal–client relationship. It should ideally be signed by the client before you agree to be retained and should outline the terms of the relationship between you and the client. In addition, the retainer agreement should be clearly explained to the client. If the language in which the retainer agreement is written is not the client's first language, it would be prudent to have an interpreter present when the retainer is explained.

A retainer agreement should include the following:

- a clear statement of the names and other identifying information about the paralegal (or firm) and client;

- a statement regarding the extent of the paralegal's licence (for example, that the paralegal is a paralegal licensed by the LSUC to practise in Ontario);

---

6 Law Society of Upper Canada (LSUC), *Practice Management Guidelines* (2009; amendments current to 2016), online: <http://www.lsuc.on.ca/For-Lawyers/Manage-Your-Practice/Representation/Client-Service/Practice-Management-Guidelines/>.

- a statement indicating that the client and paralegal have reviewed the paralegal's basic ethical obligations;
- a description of the scope of representation (for example, "for legal advice pertaining to an immigration application" or "for a consultation");
- a statement that the paralegal cannot guarantee any particular outcome with regard to the matter;
- a listing of fees and the manner in which they will be billed;
- a listing of other matters that may be billed, such as mileage, travel time, and other costs (for example, courier fees and court filing disbursements);
- a description of what (if any) financial retainer will be paid in advance of the work to be done, and how billings will be deducted from the retainer; and
- general contract terms, including a statement of governing law that makes clear that any disputes with regard to the retainer or fees are to be litigated in Ontario.

With regard to fees, if billings are done by hourly rate, then the retainer agreement should set out the hourly rates; if they are done on a contingency fee basis, the details of these arrangements should be set out. If more than one person works on the file (for example, an employee to whom work is delegated in addition to the paralegal), the hourly rates of all relevant persons should be specified. You may also include a statement to the effect that you will only bill for time reasonably and necessarily incurred, and note any maximum amounts or limits to be charged for certain tasks, if you have agreed to any. Finally, you should outline how often the client will be billed and how the bills should be paid.

As discussed earlier, under the heading "Conflicts of Interest and Identifying Clients," the term "retainer" is used to describe the advance payment made by a client that is deposited in the paralegal's trust account. A financial retainer is usually paid at the time that the retainer agreement is signed. As the paralegal bills the client for legal services rendered, the amount billed may be withdrawn from the trust account and deposited into the general account. The paralegal may request that the client replenish the retainer from time to time, as it is billed out. Insisting on a financial retainer before work is done is a prudent business practice because collecting client fees after the fact can be difficult.

For a sample retainer agreement, see Appendix 6.2 to this chapter.

Errors and Omissions Insurance

Rule 8.04 and By-Law 6, section 12(1) make it mandatory for most paralegals practising in Ontario to obtain and maintain adequate **errors and omissions insurance** (also called professional liability insurance). By-Law 6 exempts some paralegals from the obligation to maintain errors and omissions insurance, but the categories of exemptions are narrow. For example, paralegals providing legal services exclusively through clinics funded by legal aid are exempted from the requirement to maintain professional liability insurance. Paralegals working for certain not-for-profit organizations, government offices, and trade unions are also exempt from the requirement to maintain errors and omissions insurance.

errors and omissions insurance
the insurance that covers an individual licensee in the event that a client is successful in suing for professional negligence; also called professional liability insurance

Paralegals must provide written proof of their compliance with the requirement to carry errors and omissions insurance before they begin providing legal services, and they must do this annually.

The LSUC will determine what is "adequate" errors and omissions insurance from time to time. At present, section 12(1) of By-Law 6 provides that the policy limit for each single claim should be no less than $1 million, and an aggregate policy limit for all claims should be no less than $2 million per year. The by-law contains specific requirements that must be in place, for example, naming the LSUC as an additional insured for the purposes of reporting claims and receiving notice of the cancellation or amendment of the policy, and requiring 60 days' written notice to the LSUC prior to cancellation or amendment of the policy. Paralegals are required to work cooperatively with their insurers to make sure that claims against them are resolved efficiently, and are personally responsible for paying any amount of liability over that covered by their insurance. In addition, they will be required to pay deductibles that, according to section 12 of By-Law 6, must be reasonable in relation to the paralegal's financial resources.

The requirement that paralegals carry errors and omissions insurance protects clients as well as paralegals. It assures clients that they will be compensated for any successful negligence actions against their paralegals, and it assures paralegals that they will not risk losing personal assets to pay any judgments made against them. Generally, the insurer will pay the amount of any damages award made against the insured *and* the costs of defending the claim. This is important because, even in the case of groundless claims, legal fees can be very costly. Paralegals supervised by lawyers should likely maintain errors and omissions insurance of their own because, although errors made by those paralegals are covered by the lawyers' insurance policies, the contract of insurance is between the lawyer and the insurer, and it is the lawyer's vicarious liability that is covered by the policy. Thus, paralegals who are themselves defendants to an action may find that they lack coverage.

Conclusion

Paralegals have strong obligations to their clients. Clients are generally persons who consult a paralegal and on whose behalf the paralegal provides or agrees to provide legal services. However, a paralegal can incur obligations to people that he or she has not expressly taken on as clients. A person who has consulted the paralegal and reasonably concludes that the paralegal has agreed to act on his or her behalf can be a client even if the paralegal does not subjectively and expressly consent to representing him or her. You must perform all services undertaken on behalf of your clients to the standard of a competent paralegal, and should not undertake to do things that you cannot handle.

When advising clients, you must be honest and candid, and provide advice only within your permitted scope of practice. In addition, you may not knowingly assist in or encourage any dishonesty, fraud, crime, or illegal conduct when providing advice, and must take reasonable measures to avoid becoming the "tool or dupe" of an unscrupulous client or that client's associates.

When dealing with clients with a disability, you should maintain a normal professional relationship as far as is reasonably possible. If a client loses the capacity to manage his or her legal affairs, you must take steps to have a representative appointed for that client. Whenever possible on a reasonable basis, you must encourage your clients to compromise or settle a dispute. You should never draw out a matter for the purpose of creating more fees.

Identifying who the client is can be difficult. It is imperative that you make clear to all involved in a matter who is and who is not a client, particularly in cases where one party to a dispute is unrepresented. In addition, paralegals have specific obligations concerning client identification and verification of those clients' identities whether the clients are individuals or organizations. You must avoid conflicts of interest in your dealings with clients and, where this is not possible, refer clients to another paralegal or lawyer.

You must hold all information that you gain in the course of your professional relationships with clients in strict confidence indefinitely, except if you are required by law or by order of a tribunal to disclose such information. You may also disclose confidential information if doing so is necessary in order for you to defend yourself against allegations of criminal wrongdoing, malpractice, or misconduct; and if you have reasonable grounds to believe that there is an imminent risk of death or serious bodily harm to an identifiable person or group and that disclosing the information is necessary to prevent the death or harm.

Regardless of whether you are communicating by paper, by email, over the telephone, or in person, you are held to the same standards of professionalism and competence outlined in Rules 2 and 3 and related guidelines. You should be as formal in your electronic communications as you are when using more traditional forms of written communication, and should take all necessary steps to ensure the confidentiality of client information in electronic form.

To foster solid client relationships and to allow you and your clients to derive the greatest benefit from your use of technology, you should personalize voice mail messages but try to avoid using voice mail if possible; set up and maintain systems mindfully; make sure that clients are able to access your direct voice mail or email quickly, and that you pick up or read messages promptly; and ensure that you know where to draw the line in your use of technology.

Retainer agreements should be made in writing at the beginning of the paralegal–client relationship. They should outline the terms of the relationship between you and the client, and should include—among other things—a description of the scope of representation, a statement indicating that you and the client have reviewed your ethical obligations, a listing of fees and the manner in which they will be billed, and a description of what (if any) financial retainer will be paid in advance of the work to be done.

Non-engagement letters should be completed, filed, and entered into the conflicts system for all persons who have consulted the paralegal and whom the paralegal will not be representing. They should explicitly indicate the date of consultation, any applicable limitation periods, and the reason the paralegal is declining to act in the matter. Non-engagement letters must clearly state that the paralegal has not been retained in the matter. They should also recommend that the person seek other representation.

APPENDIX 6.1

Sample Non-Engagement Letter

[firm letterhead]

May 2, 20XX

Dear Mr. Smythe,

Re: Landlord and Tenant Case, Smythe v. Rains

This letter is to confirm that I am unable to provide legal services to you in the Landlord and Tenant matter we discussed in our meeting of May 1, 20XX. Scheduling conflicts with other matters I am tending to leave me unable to provide the services you require. As a result, I have recommended that you retain a different representative well before the scheduled hearing on June 23, 20XX. As a courtesy, I have provided you with a list of paralegals specializing in these types of matters. It is important that you retain a legal representative as soon as possible to ensure your matter is dealt with appropriately and to avoid delays in the proceeding.

All of your documents were returned to you at our meeting and no retainer was paid, so everything outstanding is complete.

Thank you for your interest in my services and I wish you success in the matter you face.

Yours truly,

EVANS LEGAL SERVICES

Lucas Evans

Paralegal

APPENDIX 6.2

Sample Retainer Agreement

[firm letterhead]

April 23, 20XX

Client matter no. 1234

Whistle Cleaning Inc.
222 Lakeshore Blvd.
Mississauga, Ontario
A1A 1A1

Attn.: Rosalie Bradshaw, President

Dear Ms Bradshaw,

Re: Small claims litigation against Howard Warne for breach of contract

Evans Legal Services is pleased to offer this letter as acceptance of its retainer for the matter above. Evans Legal Services is a paralegal firm. We hereby confirm that Lucas Evans, who will have carriage of this matter, is a paralegal licensed by the Law Society of Upper Canada to provide legal services in Ontario. As discussed at our initial meeting, paralegal licensees do have restrictions on their scope of practice. That said, we are satisfied that your matter falls within the authorized scope of practice of paralegals. We further confirm that the ethical obligations governing licensed paralegals in Ontario have been reviewed with you at your initial consultation meeting with Mr. Lucas Evans on April 21, 20XX.

GOVERNING LAW & FORUM SELECTION
This agreement is governed by the law of Ontario, and disputes concerning this agreement will be resolved in the courts of Ontario.

CLIENT GOALS
Whistle Cleaning Inc. ("the client") wishes to obtain from this litigation the following:

1. full payment of amounts not tendered for services rendered;
2. pre-judgment interest dating back to [date] in the amount of [percentage]
3. post-judgment interest as set by the court; and
4. all legal costs awarded against Defendant up to 15% of claim.

While we will do our utmost to achieve the client's goals, it is important to note that the decision of the judge in this matter may be affected by matters that are not within our control, for example, evidence produced by your opponent in the action.

SERVICES TO BE PROVIDED
Upon your instructions, the following steps will be taken on your matter:

INITIATION PHASE
1. Drafting of Plaintiff's Claim
2. Collection of detailed facts of the case and drafting of Schedule A to the claim
3. Filing of Plaintiff's Claim with Small Claims Court in Brampton, Ontario
4. Service of Plaintiff's Claim upon Defendant
5. Receipt of Defence and any potential Defendant's Claim
6. Receipt of Notice of Settlement Conference

SETTLEMENT CONFERENCE PHASE (MANDATORY)
1. Review of Defence and accompanying evidence and development of Plaintiff strategy
2. Legal research as required
3. Settlement Conference preparation session with client (1 hour)
4. Representation at Settlement Conference

TRIAL PHASE (IF NECESSARY)
1. Identification, securing, and preparation of witnesses
2. Preparation of necessary trial materials (evidence book, book of authorities, etc.)
3. Trial preparation session with client (1 hour)
4. Representation at trial (minimum 2 hours, $100.00/hr for each additional hour)

FEE SCHEDULE & BILLING
This provision of legal services shall be conducted on a flat-fee basis. The client agrees to pay Evans Legal Services the sum of $350.00 upon completion of the Initiation Phase and receipt of invoice. All legal fees are subject to HST. The remainder of the fees shall be paid as follows:

1. The sum of $350.00 for the cost of the Settlement Conference Phase
2. The sum of $750.00 for the cost of the Trial Phase

Invoices not paid within 30 days of the date of the invoice will be subject to 2% interest until paid.

DISBURSEMENTS AND FILING FEES
The client agrees to pay all required court fees, including the $95.00 filing fee in respect of the Plaintiff's Claim. The client also agrees to reimburse Evans Legal Services for any reasonable and necessary costs associated with preparing and executing the claim, including photocopying, mailing, courier costs, extraneous travel, and parking. All these expenses will be clearly detailed, and significant expenses will be confirmed with the client prior to being made. Some disbursements may be subject to HST.

CLIENT INSTRUCTIONS
This letter confirms that Rosalie Bradshaw is charged solely with giving instructions to Evans Legal Services on how to proceed at any and all stages of the case.

CLIENT COMMUNICATION

This letter confirms that Evans Legal Services will keep the client fully informed about progress on the matter through email and telephone communications as necessary. Likewise, the client confirms that she will keep Evans Legal Services fully informed about issues pertaining to the case.

SETTLEMENT FUNDS

In the event the matter settles, settlement funds shall be payable to Evans Legal Services in trust. If the settlement funds are payable to you, any outstanding fees and disbursements may be invoiced and deducted from these funds before the balance of the funds is paid to the client.

CLIENT CONFIDENTIALITY AND CONFLICTS OF INTEREST

Throughout all stages of this legal process and for all times after, Evans Legal Services and I, Lucas Evans, undertake to keep all of the client's information in strict confidence subject to any exceptions allowed under the Law Society of Upper Canada's *Paralegal Rules of Conduct*. Furthermore, I undertake not to engage in any activity that is or could be perceived to be in conflict with the interests of the client.

TERMINATION OF LEGAL SERVICES

The client is entitled to terminate this agreement and Evans Legal Services' representation of the client by providing written notice of the termination.

Evans Legal Services is entitled to terminate its representation of the client for good reasons, including, but not limited to, the following:

(a)   the client's failure to pay accounts when rendered;

(b)   the client's failure to cooperate with Evans Legal Services in any reasonable request;

(c)   the client's failure to provide instructions; or

(d)   if continuing to act would be unethical.

In the event of the termination of this agreement the client is responsible for paying fees and disbursements incurred prior to the termination of the agreement.

_____   Date: _____

Evans Legal Services per Lucas Evans

_____   Date: _____

Whistle Cleaning Inc. per Rosalie Bradshaw

KEY TERMS

client, 78
competent paralegal, 78
confidential information, 81
conflict of interest, 84
errors and omissions insurance, 93
independent legal advice/independent legal
  representation, 86
non-engagement letter, 88
phantom client, 87
Professionalism Hours, 79
retainer, 84
retainer agreement, 88
retainer letter, 88
Substantive Hours, 79
transaction with a client, 84

USEFUL URLS

Law Society of British Columbia. 2016. General Retainer
    Agreement. <http://www.lawsociety.bc.ca/docs/
    practice/resources/retainer-general.pdf>.

Law Society of Upper Canada (LSUC). 2009. *Practice
    Management Guidelines*. <http://www.lsuc.on.ca/
    For-Lawyers/Manage-Your-Practice/Representation/
    Client-Service/Practice-Management-Guidelines/>.

Lawyers' Professional Indemnity Company (LAWPRO).
    2017. "Precedent Documents and Retainers." <http://
    www.practicepro.ca/practice/
    financesbookletprecedents.asp>.

Rolph, Debra. 2014. "LAWPRO Tales of Horror: The
    Phantom Client Returns ... Again and Again." <http://
    avoidaclaim.com/2014/lawpro-tales-of-horror
    -the-phantom-client-returns-again-and-again/>.

Solove, Daniel J. *The Future of Reputation: Gossip, Rumor,
    and Privacy on the Internet*. New Haven, CT: Yale
    University Press, 2007. <http://docs.law.gwu.edu/
    facweb/dsolove/Future-of-Reputation/text.htm>.

Wertz, Glenda. 2004. "The Ins and Outs of Errors and
    Omissions Insurance." *Insurance Journal*, July 19, 2004.
    <http://www.insurancejournal.com/magazines/
    west/2004/07/19/features/44745.htm>.

REVIEW QUESTIONS

1. Who is a client?

2. To what standard are paralegals required to provide services undertaken on behalf of their clients? Explain the meaning of the standard.

3. Explain the duty of confidentiality.

4. What is a conflict of interest?

5. What must paralegals keep in mind when communicating electronically with clients and others?

6. Can paralegals share their email lists (that is, the email addresses of their clients and business contacts) with advertisers in exchange for financial compensation?

7. When should a paralegal send a non-engagement letter?

8. What is a phantom client?

9. What steps must be taken to verify the identity of a client that is a corporation?

10. What steps must be taken to verify the identity of a client who is an individual?

11. Which by-law should you consult to determine what independent source documents are acceptable for use when verifying the identity of a client who is an individual?

12. What is the amount of errors and omissions insurance that practising paralegals, other than exempt paralegals, are required to carry?

13. How many hours of continuing professional development are paralegals required to engage in each year? How many of these hours are to be Substantive Hours? How many of these are to be Professionalism Hours?

14. What is the difference between a retainer agreement and a retainer letter?

15. Can paralegals who use collection agencies to collect outstanding accounts provide the client's complete file to the collection agency? Cite the authority for your answer.

16. What are some limits on the paralegal's obligation to maintain client confidentiality? Cite the authority for your answer.

17. Is the LSUC required to accredit the Professionalism Hours required as part of paralegals' continuing professional development?

18. If a paralegal represents a bank, is that paralegal permitted to take out a loan from that institution?

SCENARIO-BASED QUESTIONS

1. Partying Paralegal

Fred Flynn, a licensed paralegal, whose Toronto-based practice deals exclusively with workplace injuries, is attending a friend's pool party. While at the party he chats with Sue Simone, who tells him all about her upcoming trial for speeding in a school zone. Sue is certain that she was not going 25 km over the speed limit, as the officer who stopped her claimed. Fred, who thinks Sue is very attractive, is an attentive listener. Sue asks Fred for his phone number, which makes Fred very happy. He gives Sue his business card, which contains his cell phone number. Sue does not call Fred until a month later. When she calls she is angry because her trial in the provincial offences matter is being held at 9 a.m. and she was expecting Fred to be there as her representative. Discuss some of the issues posed by this scenario and the steps Fred should have taken to avoid this situation. Cite any relevant Rules, Guidelines, and By-Laws in support of your answer.

2. Identification Information

Tara Mickleson is a licensed paralegal. Her Kitchener, Ontario-based practice handles Small Claims Court and provincial offences matters. Clyde Bonner, an 18-year-old student who lives in Cambridge, Ontario, has consulted Tara about a street-racing ticket. He has decided to retain Tara to represent him in that matter. Tara asks Clyde for his driver's licence in order to verify his identity. Clyde produces a licence, then apologizes to Tara and asks her to return it to him because it is the fake ID that he uses to get into bars in order to be served alcohol. Next he produces his actual driver's licence for the purposes of client verification. What should Tara do? Cite any relevant Rules, Guidelines, and By-Laws in support of your answer.

3. A Quiet Chat

Timothy Taylor, a licensed paralegal, brings a field placement student, Walter O'Reilly, with him to observe him in provincial offences court for a full day. On the subway ride back to the office from the courthouse Timothy asks Walter to discuss his observations. Clinging to the pole in the crowded subway car, Walter, speaking quietly, begins his summary with a compliment, saying that he thought Timothy did a great job negotiating a plea in the case of Madelaine Evans, a school bus driver who would have lost her job for sure if there had been a conviction on the original charge. Is there a problem with Walter and Timothy's quiet chat about the client's situation? If so, what could Timothy and Walter have done differently? Cite any relevant Rules, Guidelines, and By-Laws in support of your answer.

Practice Management

7

LEARNING OUTCOMES

After completing this chapter, you should be able to:

- Understand what is meant by professional responsibility for legal services providers in Ontario as set out in Rule 8.01(1).

- Understand what is required from paralegals in terms of financial responsibility pursuant to Rule 8.01(2).

- Understand the scope of paralegals' supervisory responsibility under Rule 8.01(3), Guideline 18, and By-Law 7.1.

- Understand when and how it is appropriate for paralegals to delegate duties under Rule 8.01(4), Guideline 18, and By-Law 7.1.

- Strategically determine effective, efficient, and ethical ways to delegate tasks to employees.

Professional Responsibility

Rule 8.01 of the LSUC's *Paralegal Rules of Conduct*[1] requires paralegals to assume professional responsibility for all business with which they are entrusted. This means that they are responsible for everything that happens in their practice, including the actions of their staff. **Professional responsibility** refers to paralegals' obligations to observe the rules and **ethics** of the paralegal profession as set out in the *Law Society Act*[2] and the Rules.

For example, section 8 of Guideline 8 of the LSUC's *Paralegal Professional Conduct Guidelines*[3] clearly indicates that it is the paralegal's responsibility to ensure that his or her employees and anyone else involved with the client's matter understand the duty of confidentiality (discussed in Chapter 6). It further provides that if someone employed by the paralegal discloses confidential information without the client's authorization or in a way that is not permitted by the Rules, the paralegal will be held responsible for that breach of the duty of confidentiality. Section 20 of the same guideline again emphasizes that it is the paralegal's obligation to ensure that all staff understand their obligations with respect to confidentiality.

professional responsibility
refers to paralegals' obligations to observe the rules and ethics of the paralegal profession as determined by the LSUC

ethics
a branch of philosophy that seeks to address questions about morality; a codified set of moral rules specific to the performance of professional obligations

Supervisory Responsibility

Professionalism requires accountability and acceptance of responsibility. "Passing the buck" is *not* professional; **professionals** should not try to fault subordinates or others for their own mistakes. Rule 8 effectively codifies Harry Truman's famous statement "the buck stops here" with reference to paralegals and their work. Rule 8.01(3) and Guideline 18 provide that paralegals must directly supervise staff and assistants to whom tasks and functions are delegated. This means that, once they are licensed and practising as a paralegal, not only may they not blame their employees for their own mistakes, they must also take responsibility for mistakes that their employees make, because they are responsible for supervising them.

professional
a member of a vocation founded upon specialized education and training and subject to standards of competence and ethics

For the purposes of liability with reference to both LSUC disciplinary proceedings and civil proceedings that may be brought by clients for professional negligence, Rule 8.01(3) means that *it is no defence* for a paralegal to blame mistakes or omissions on staff. The public policy behind this rule is to protect the public from untrained or irresponsible people providing legal services. When unlicensed staff work for a paralegal, it is that paralegal's licence on the line.

The obligation to supervise requires that paralegals structure their practice in such a way that the paralegals can monitor the work of their staff members to ensure that it is done correctly, promptly, and effectively. This may mean that paralegals should approve all correspondence and court documents before these leave their office.

---

1   Law Society of Upper Canada, *Paralegal Rules of Conduct* (1 October 2014; amendments current to 2017), online: <http://www.lsuc.on.ca/paralegal-conduct-rules/>.

2   RSO 1990, c L.8.

3   Law Society of Upper Canada, *Paralegal Professional Conduct Guidelines* (1 October 2014; amendments current to 2016), online: <http://www.lsuc.on.ca/paralegal-conduct-guidelines/>.

Paralegals should hold regular meetings to answer any questions that staff may have and to receive updates on ongoing matters.

> Some paralegals also choose to accept Ontario paralegal students as field placement students. Ontario paralegal students are required to perform a minimum of 120 hours of field placement prior to licensing (see By-Law 4, section 11(1)). If a paralegal has agreed to accept and to supervise a field placement student, the paralegal assumes responsibility for the work performed by the Ontario paralegal student.

Delegation

The paralegal's supervisory responsibility extends to hiring and training staff. While paralegals are responsible for supervising their employees, they are not required to do everything themselves. As a paralegal's business grows, he or she will need to **delegate**—that is, assign tasks to others—in a manner that is effective and that allows him or her to properly oversee the work of others.

delegate
to assign tasks to others

Delegating may not come naturally to many entrepreneurs, but appropriate delegation of tasks is critical to the success of many small businesses. Appropriate delegation of work and authority may boost morale; staff are often more likely to work harder and feel more personally invested in the success of a business when they can take initiative. In addition, delegating can allow the paralegal to spend more time outside work and avoid burnout.

Paralegals who work in businesses large enough to sustain employees should delegate enough work and authority to ensure that tasks are completed in a timely fashion. In many areas of practice, the provision of legal services involves a good deal of detailed paperwork, administrative work, and other tasks. Preparing court documents can involve many hours of photocopying and assembling. Office administration—including banking and paying bills, and purchasing supplies—involves many time-consuming tasks. It may be difficult for paralegals to fulfill the professional duties for which they were trained if they are faced with a mountain of paperwork and odd jobs to complete, and they may find that it makes more financial sense for them to delegate such tasks to others.

Guideline 18 sets out general advice with respect to delegation of tasks to support staff, including limits on the type of work that can be delegated and the degree of supervision required. Section 5 of the guideline provides that paralegals should be satisfied with respect to the competence of the person to whom they are delegating tasks—in other words, with the staff member's experience, training, and skills. In addition, paralegal employers must ensure that they hire and train staff properly. This includes obtaining information about potential employees to assess their competence and trustworthiness. Paralegals may conduct criminal records checks and credit checks prior to hiring employees, and are required to confirm the information contained in the candidate's resumé by consulting references and verifying previous employment prior to offering a position to a candidate.

Any unlicensed employees to whom tasks are delegated must clearly identify themselves as such in all written and verbal communications.

According to section 6 of Guideline 18, a paralegal's staff must be aware of the following:

- the types of tasks that will and will not be delegated;
- what sort of conduct with respect to courtesy and professionalism is and is not appropriate;
- the definitions of discrimination and harassment, and the fact that such conduct is prohibited;
- the definition and scope of the duty to maintain client confidentiality, and methods to ensure that confidentiality is not breached;
- the definition and scope of what might constitute a conflict of interest, and how to use the conflict-checking system;
- how to handle client property, including money and other items, properly; and
- how to keep records properly.

Guideline 18 refers to By-Law 7.1[4] and Rule 8.01(1), (3), (4), and (5). Both By-Law 7.1 and Rule 8.01 make clear that there are tasks that *cannot* be properly delegated to support staff. According to By-Law 7.1, support staff may not give legal advice, conduct negotiations, sign important correspondence, or forward to a client documents that have not been reviewed by the supervising paralegal. Rule 8.01(4) prohibits non-licensee staff from providing legal services, being held out as licensees, or performing any of the duties that only paralegals may perform or doing things that paralegals themselves may not do.

Although paralegals may delegate certain tasks, they remain ultimately responsible for ensuring that those tasks are completed properly. To enable paralegals to meet this responsibility, By-Law 7.1, section 1(1) provides that paralegals retain effective control over any non-licensee's provision of services. "Effective control" means that the licensee may, without the agreement of the non-licensee, take any action necessary to ensure that the licensee complies with the *Law Society Act*; the By-Laws; and the LSUC's Rules, Guidelines, and policies (By-Law 7.1, section 1(2)). Paralegals must have a direct relationship with each client, meaning that the client retains the paralegal and that support staff are not parties to the retainer agreement. Rule 8.01 restates the requirement that paralegals assume complete professional responsibility for all business entrusted to them.

Licensed paralegals may wish to "team up" with professionals from other disciplines, such as accountants and tax consultants, to serve a wider range of client needs. By-Law 7, sections 17 and 18 allow for such partnerships to support or supplement the provision of legal services only where the business is operated as a **multi-discipline partnership**. All multi-discipline partnerships must obtain approval from the LSUC.

The by-law also sets limits on the delegation of tasks among professionals working in multi-discipline partnerships. Each professional within such a partnership may only provide the services for which he or she has been trained and is licensed.

multi-discipline partnership
a partnership of licensees and other professionals, such as accountants and tax consultants, through which paralegals can provide their clients with non-legal professional services that support the provision of legal services

---

4   Law Society of Upper Canada, By-Law 7.1 (25 October 2007, editorial changes 2 March 2017), online: <https://www.lsuc.on.ca/by-laws/>.

The licensee partners—paralegals and lawyers—are responsible for the actions of the non-licensee partners and must ensure that they have obtained professional liability insurance. Paralegals remain accountable to the LSUC for the work of the other professionals with whom they practise (see By-Law 7, part III; Rule 8.01(5); and Guideline 18, section 4).

Even when the following are carried out by employees, By-Law 7.1 makes it clear that paralegals are responsible for

- all services rendered,
- all communications made, and
- all materials prepared

on behalf of their business.

Strategically Delegating Duties

Using various outsourced services and entering into contracts with other businesses can allow sole practitioners to enhance their business success. Sole practitioners might consider using answering services, cleaning services, or occasional information support services to make their businesses run more smoothly. They might also consider delegating certain tasks to professionals who are more highly skilled in certain circumstances—for example, contracting with a lawyer or obtaining legal research from an outside source in a relatively complex case.

Time management is an important part of the ongoing business planning process. This includes scheduling appointments, diarizing due dates, and setting aside time to prepare documents and to complete other tasks. Paralegals, especially sole practitioners, should document how their time is spent for billing purposes as well as to assess efficiency, noting how much time was spent on client work (billable time) and how much was spent on administrative tasks (non-billable time). If delegating administrative tasks to others will free up more billable time, this will improve the business's profitability.

To delegate tasks effectively, paralegals should do the following:

- Determine what work should be delegated.
- Give clear instructions—be clear and precise about employees' responsibilities, the desired results, and any specific methods required to complete the tasks.
- Have a system in place to review employees' work.
- Be specific in explaining what types of decisions employees have the authority to make in the course of performing their tasks, and make clear that they should check with the supervising paralegal before stepping outside of that authority.
- Make sure that employees are aware that they should ask questions or request assistance if they are uncertain of what to do.
- Ensure that employees understand what has been assigned to them. It may be useful to have them repeat their assignments back to you in their own words.

Although the paralegal is ultimately responsible to clients for all work he or she delegates, employees will often perform better if they are made to *feel* they are responsible, and if they feel a sense of ownership and accomplishment with regard to their work. Training is an investment—helping employees grow professionally will pay off in the long term as they are able to undertake more complex tasks.

Financial Responsibility

Rule 8.01(2) and Guideline 23 require paralegals to meet the financial obligations incurred in the course of their practice on behalf of clients "promptly." The exception is where a paralegal has indicated clearly in writing to the person to whom the debt is owed that it is *not* to be the paralegal's personal obligation.

The requirement to deal with financial obligations "promptly" means that money owed should be paid without undue delay. While delay is unavoidable in some cases, paralegals must not cause or contribute to the delay.

Interestingly, section 4 of Guideline 23 provides that if the client changes representatives after the original paralegal has retained someone such as an expert witness, but before that person has been paid for his or her services, it is the original paralegal who should take steps to inform him or her of the change in representatives. The original paralegal should supply the full contact information of the client's new representative to the person to whom the financial obligation is owed.

By-Law 9 and Rule 3.07 govern related issues of financial transactions and records, and client property, respectively; Guidelines 10 and 15 provide interpretative advice regarding the interaction of these rules.

Books and Records—By-Law 9

By-Law 9 outlines paralegals' accounting obligations: part I of the by-law is concerned with definitions and interpretation of the by-law; part II of the by-law governs the handling of money by bankrupt licensees; part II.1 of the by-law governs the handling of money by licensees whose licences are suspended; part III of the by-law discusses cash transactions; part IV of the by-law deals with trust account transactions; and part V of the by-law deals with record-keeping requirements. In part V, section 18 requires paralegals to keep detailed records of all financial transactions relating to all money and other property received and disbursed in connection with their professional businesses. Section 19 sets out specific record-keeping requirements when paralegals receive cash. It is important for paralegals to familiarize themselves with the contents of By-Law 9 and to review *The Bookkeeping Guide for Paralegals* published by the LSUC for more information.[5] Paralegals may require the assistance of a bookkeeper or accountant in order to ensure that they are in compliance.

---

5   Law Society of Upper Canada, *The Bookkeeping Guide for Paralegals* (2015), online: <https://www.lsuc.on.ca/uploadedFiles/PDC/Practice_Management/Paralegals_Only/Paralegal%20Bookkeeping%20Guide%20FINAL-s.pdf>.

Client Funds—Trust Accounting

According to section 7 of By-Law 9, paralegals have special obligations when handling client funds. Client funds means money that belongs to the client, not to the paralegal. Most commonly, paralegals will hold client funds in trust if the client pays the paralegal a financial retainer in advance of work and billing for a matter; until the paralegal has completed the work and billed the client, this money belongs to the client and must be held in trust. To recover fees from the client's funds in trust, the paralegal is obliged to render an account to the client. Once the services have been performed and the account has been delivered to the client, the paralegal may transfer funds from the trust account to the firm's **general account** in respect of those fees. In contrast, as soon as disbursements such as court filing fees have been incurred, the paralegal is entitled to deduct the cost of those disbursements from the trust account. Paralegals must still render accounts in respect of those disbursements and must clearly distinguish between fees and disbursements in those accounts, but they need not wait until those bills have been prepared and sent to the client before transferring funds from the trust account to the firm's general account. Review "Planning for Practice: Trust in Me?" to determine whether the paralegal in that scenario obeyed the Rules concerning moneys received in trust.

general account
a firm's operating account that contains money belonging to the firm; funds held in that account will be used to pay bills owed by the firm

PLANNING FOR PRACTICE

Trust in Me?

A Toronto homeowner filed a small claims lawsuit against a local pest control company, claiming a full refund and damages suffered as a result of what she called "shoddy work" in treating her home for a termite infestation. She claimed the company was not forthright and honest with her and didn't make a full effort to exterminate the pests. She had intended to sell her house and move to the United States, but she claimed the company's failure to get rid of the termites resulted in a sale falling through, costing her significant amounts of money.

The company, for its part, insisted it fully provided the service it was contracted for, using the chemicals and techniques it was legally allowed to use under federal law. The pest company also claimed that the homeowner failed to follow instructions for post-treatment care of the home in her haste to prepare the house for sale, necessitating further treatments.

The company contacted James Viola, a licensed paralegal since 2013, to represent it in the case. Viola accepted a $1,650 retainer for services and disbursements. Under terms of the retainer agreement, a flat fee of $500 would be paid at each of the three stages of the case—initiation, settlement conference, and trial. If the trial were to run longer than anticipated, an additional retainer would be provided.

The following morning, Viola deposited the retained cheque into his firm's trust account.

Time to respond to the plaintiff's claim was short, so Viola prepared and filed a simple defence pleading to meet the 20-day deadline. That pleading would later be amended to detail a more vigorous defence.

> Viola provided his client with an invoice for his fees at the first stage, detailing the actions he had taken. He provided a second invoice for disbursements made on the client's behalf.
>
> The next day, he transferred the amount of both invoices to his firm's general account.
>
> The mandatory settlement conference was scheduled for a month later and Viola worked diligently with his client to prepare for that conference, including assembling, printing, and serving the book of documents.
>
> During the settlement conference, there was considerable back-and-forth between the parties. The deputy judge presiding became convinced no settlement could be reached so he ordered the case to trial. He also ordered both sides to produce more documents to support their cases.
>
> Viola became concerned about mounting out-of-pocket expenses so he decided to bill clients more quickly to be paid sooner. He provided an invoice to the client for disbursements. He also prepared one for his fees but held off sending that one so he could double-check it against his tickler system.
>
> The next morning, he transferred the amount of both invoices to the firm's general account. That evening when he was tying up loose ends, he emailed the client with the invoice for the fees.
>
> The plaintiff failed to set a trial date with the court and eventually the case was dismissed as abandoned. Viola refunded the remaining retainer funds to the client.
>
> Do you believe Viola handled the accounting in this matter correctly based on the retainer agreement and the Rules?

trust account
a separate account that paralegals must maintain to keep client funds held in trust

Paralegals might also hold client funds in trust to facilitate payment of a settlement. Trust money must be kept separate and apart from the paralegal's other business accounts in a separate **trust account**. Although a paralegal may have more than one trust account, that paralegal will usually have just one in which he or she holds client funds for numerous clients. The paralegal must maintain scrupulous records of any transactions involving his or her trust account(s), keeping track of how much money belongs to each client and leaving an accounting trail of all moneys transferred between the trust account and his or her own account that is easy to follow. By-Law 9, section 9 outlines those specific obligations.

Trust accounts must be controlled by the paralegal who holds the moneys in trust. That paralegal is ultimately responsible for any inappropriate withdrawal of client trust funds, and access to the trust account by employees should be restricted. The paralegal should never sign blank trust cheques or allow others to access blank trust account cheques or electronic banking. It is preferable for signing authority to be granted only to other licensees.

Paralegals should take their financial obligations very seriously. In two recent cases, *Law Society of Upper Canada v Lee* and *Law Society of Upper Canada v Koroma*, below, the Law Society Tribunal granted motions seeking immediate interlocutory suspension of the paralegals' licences.

In *Law Society of Upper Canada v Lee*, 2016 ONLSTH 44, the tribunal indicated that there was clear evidence that money obtained from a client in trust and deposited in a trust account had been used to operate the paralegal's business. The tribunal stated, at paragraph 33: "Misappropriation is very serious misconduct for lawyers and paralegals, given the trust that members of the public must have in those to whom they entrust their money. The public cannot have confidence in the administration of justice if a licensee who appears to have misappropriated funds continues to provide legal services."

In *Law Society of Upper Canada v Koroma*, 2016 ONLSTH 46, the LSUC, in the course of an investigation, received correspondence from the paralegal in which the paralegal admitted to having mishandled and misappropriated trust funds. The tribunal stated, at paragraph 33: "In this case, the evidence of misappropriation is clear and undisputed, and moreover, the Licensee has not provided access to information about his trust accounts so that the Law Society can investigate whether there are other issues. Misappropriation and dishonesty are at the most serious end of the spectrum of misconduct for lawyers and paralegals, given the trust that each members [*sic*] of the public must have in those to whom they entrust their money. The public cannot have confidence in the administration of justice when a person who has admitted to taking money that did not belong to him and has not provided information about it, [*sic*] continues to provide legal services."

While these were both interlocutory suspensions of licences, these cases demonstrate the importance the LSUC places upon the paralegal's ethical obligations with respect to financial accounting and handling of clients' funds.

In another recent case, *Law Society of Upper Canada v Yau*, 2016 ONLSTH 41, the paralegal was the subject of a practice management review that discovered that the paralegal was in breach of several provisions of By-Law 9. The paralegal collected fees for services to be rendered in the future but did not deposit those moneys in a trust account, did not render accounts before depositing those sums into a general account, and did not maintain trust, general receipts, or disbursement journals. The licensee did not maintain client trust ledger cards, prepare monthly trust reconciliations, or complete trust comparisons as required. The paralegal was given specific direction concerning his financial accounting obligations and, sometime later, a follow-up practice management review was conducted. At that time, it was determined that the paralegal had taken no steps to comply with the LSUC's directives concerning financial accounting. The paralegal and the LSUC consented to a court order that directed the paralegal to comply with his obligations pursuant to By-Law 9. When it was not able to schedule a follow-up audit to ensure that the paralegal was in compliance with this court order, the LSUC commenced an investigation that revealed continued accounting irregularities. The paralegal admitted that his continued breach of By-Law 9 constituted professional misconduct. The tribunal suspended the paralegal's licence for a period of five months, with that suspension continuing indefinitely until the paralegal could demonstrate that he was in compliance with both the order and the by-law. The paralegal was also ordered to pay up to $4,800 to fund a further practice review by the LSUC and to pay $15,000 in costs as the tribunal accepted the parties' joint submission on penalty. A joint submission on penalty generally indicates that the parties are cooperating, so it is feasible that in a similar case where a paralegal was not cooperating with the LSUC, a greater penalty would be imposed.

Cash Transactions

Paralegals must be very careful when accepting cash from clients. Paralegals may not receive more than $7,500 in cash for any client file (By-Law 9, section 4(1)). This restriction aims to prevent money laundering and payment with the proceeds of crime. If a client does not have a chequing account, a paralegal should ask for payment by money order or cashier's cheque.

Paralegals should be careful and detail-oriented with respect to their financial obligations—or they will very likely face severe professional consequences from the LSUC.

Client Property

As mentioned above, Rule 3.07 and Guideline 10 address client property. A paralegal is required to care for that property as a careful and prudent owner would. The rule and guideline emphasize the paralegal's role as a fiduciary. While the client's property is in the paralegal's custody, that property must be distinguishable from property owned by the paralegal. The paralegal must also maintain records necessary to identify the property as the client's property. These records are often known as client property ledgers. Another type of record is the valuable property record mandated by Guideline 10, which applies to items that can be sold or negotiated by the paralegal. The client's property is to be returned promptly upon the client's request or at the termination of the retainer.

The Client File

Rule 3.07 also applies to documents provided to the paralegal by the client and to documents that are "created or collected by the paralegal for the client's benefit" during the paralegal–client relationship (Guideline 10, section 4). According to Guideline 10, the jurisprudence developed by the courts on the issue of ownership of client files as between lawyers and clients may, in future, be applied to paralegals. Section 5 of the guideline lists a number of documents that belong to the client. Some items included on the list may come as a surprise, for example, copies of case law, but, in general, anything generated for the client, paid for by the client, or documenting dealings on behalf of the client with persons other than the client is included in the list. Specifically excluded from this list are documents such as notes or memoranda of meetings or telephone calls with the client (Guideline 10, section 6). One rationale for this exclusion is obvious: the client was a party to those conversations and could have taken and kept his or her own notes. In addition, if a client should file a complaint against a licensee, the original notes concerning conversations with that client would be in the licensee's possession and could be furnished to the LSUC investigators by that licensee.

Upon termination of the retainer by the client, it is the documents that belong to the client that must be provided to the client. Section 7 of the guideline notes that a paralegal should retain copies of client documents, at his or her own cost, to defend against future complaints or claims.

Conclusion

As professionals, paralegals are responsible for their own actions in their practices as well as for the actions of their staff. Ultimately, a paralegal assumes professional responsibility for all business with which he or she is entrusted.

Paralegals should take all financial obligations incurred in the course of the practice very seriously, meeting all such obligations promptly unless the paralegal has indicated clearly in writing to the person to whom the debt is owed that it is not to be the paralegal's personal obligation.

Paralegals are responsible for supervising their employees and must assume responsibility for any mistakes that those employees make. With respect to liability with reference to LSUC disciplinary proceedings and civil proceedings, it is no defence to blame mistakes or omissions on staff.

As a paralegal's business grows, he or she will need to delegate work to others. This can allow that paralegal to spend more time fulfilling the professional duties for which he or she was trained. For employees, delegation of work and authority may boost morale; staff will feel more personally invested in the success of a business if they are able to take initiative. The Guidelines explain what kind of work can be delegated and the degree of supervision required. Certain tasks cannot be properly delegated to staff, as described in the By-Laws and Rules.

Paralegals must ensure that they hire and train all staff properly, and that they are satisfied with respect to the experience, training, and skills of the person to whom they are delegating tasks. All unlicensed employees to whom tasks are delegated must clearly identify themselves as such in all written and verbal communications.

Paralegals may team up with professionals from other disciplines, such as accountants and tax consultants, in multi-discipline partnerships in order to serve a wider range of client needs. All multi-discipline partnerships must obtain approval from the LSUC. Each professional in such a partnership may only provide to clients the services for which he or she has been trained and is licensed; paralegals remain accountable to the LSUC for the work of the other professionals with whom they practise.

Training employees is an investment. By helping them grow professionally, paralegals will benefit from the new skills their employees acquire.

KEY TERMS

USEFUL URLS

Yoskovitz, Ben. 2006. "The Secret to Successfully Delegating Work in 6 Steps." <http://www.instigatorblog.com/the-secret-to-successfully-delegating-work-in-6-steps/2006/09/01/>.

REVIEW QUESTIONS

1. What is professional responsibility?

2. What is a trust account, and what are the obligations of paralegals with respect to client funds held in trust?

3. What is a paralegal's supervisory responsibility and how does this relate to liability for errors and omissions on the part of staff?

4. Describe some steps a paralegal should take in delegating tasks.

5. Should a paralegal deposit retainer fees paid for future services to his or her general account?

6. What is a valuable property record?

7. What is the maximum amount of cash that a paralegal can accept from a client who wishes to pay his or her account in cash?

8. What degree of care must the paralegal take in respect of client property?

9. Which of the following items are client property?

   a. notes taken by the paralegal during her conversation with her client

   b. emails sent by the paralegal to an opposing paralegal

   c. letters sent by the paralegal to expert witnesses

   d. photographs taken by the paralegal at the scene of an accident in a *Highway Traffic Act* matter

   e. b, c, and d

10. Refer to By-Law 7.1 to determine which of the following tasks may be delegated to non-licensees.

   a. accepting a retainer

   b. appearing for the paralegal on a routine scheduling matter

   c. signing of all correspondence on behalf of the paralegal

   d. giving an undertaking on behalf of the paralegal

   e. sending of collection letters

SCENARIO-BASED QUESTIONS

1. **Rhonda's Rubber Stamp**

   Rhonda Lemming is a practising paralegal and a sole practitioner. Rhonda has been licensed for three years, and has had the good fortune to hire an extremely experienced law clerk, Sally Marino, to work for her. Rhonda is acting for the plaintiff in a Small Claims Court action and will be out of the office for three days. Rhonda tells Sally to prepare a batch of final reporting letters for clients while she is away and says that she trusts Sally to "rubber stamp" them with Rhonda's signature. Rhonda is surprised when Sally refuses to do that. Why does Sally refuse? Cite the relevant section(s) of the Rules, Guidelines, and By-Laws.

2. **Student Supervision**

   Alexander Bartokoff is a licensed paralegal who has agreed to supervise Melanie Wilson during her four-week placement at his firm. Melanie misses two days of her placement due to illness, but at the end of the four-week period Melanie presents her supervisor with dockets for those two days. Melanie tells Alexander that on those days and while she was ill she worked at home, conducting legal research in order to prepare a research memo. Alexander Bartokoff refuses to sign dockets for those days because she was not in the office and he had not instructed her to work from home. He is expecting Melanie to make up the two missed days at the end of her placement, but Melanie wants to attend convocation with her classmates. Returning to placement for two days will require Melanie to wait another three months until the next convocation is held, and her grandmother is flying in from England to attend the ceremony. Without those dockets, Melanie has completed only 118 hours of field placement work. Melanie does not understand why Alexander won't just sign the dockets. Explain his refusal. How many additional hours does Melanie need to complete to satisfy the LSUC's field placement requirement? Cite the relevant Rules, Guidelines, and By-Laws.

File Management and Time Management

8

LEARNING OUTCOMES

After completing this chapter, you should be able to:

- Appreciate the importance of client confidentiality.

- Understand how to maintain client confidentiality by using proper systems for file management.

- Describe how to effectively and efficiently use systems and tools, including checklists and ticklers, to manage files.

- Understand how to use and maintain time dockets effectively.

- Plan for effective organization of file contents.

- Understand how to manage clients' property according to Rule 3.07.

- Understand how to store active client files.

- Understand how to close and store inactive client files.

Confidentiality

The LSUC's *Paralegal Rules of Conduct*,[1] as well as a long history of legal tradition, provide that effective legal advice requires full and unreserved communication between the client and counsel. Confidentiality facilitates this communication. Paralegals must hold all information relayed to them by clients in the course of their professional relationships in strict confidence. Following the best practices outlined below will assist you in complying with this requirement.

Preserve Privilege if Possible

solicitor–client privilege
privilege extended to communications between lawyers and their clients where legal advice is sought or provided and when the parties to the communication intend that information to be confidential; the concept of privilege means that the lawyer cannot be compelled to disclose the information as evidence; privilege belongs to the client

Although confidentiality and **solicitor–client privilege** are distinct concepts, there are important links between them. Client information can cease to be confidential if it is ordered into court because it is found *not* to be privileged.

In *Chancey v Dharmadi*,[2] a master determined that communications between paralegals and their clients could be determined to be privileged on a case-by-case basis. This case suggested that, in the future, privilege might be extended to licensed paralegals as a class. However, ten years after this decision, it is still not clear whether a privilege similar to solicitor–client privilege will be extended to paralegals as a class.

> In a recent decision, *Law Society of Upper Canada v Koroma*, 2016 ONLSTH 46, the LSUC redacted an affidavit sworn by its forensic auditor to eliminate privileged information. The tribunal was not called upon to determine whether those portions of the affidavit were privileged because the paralegal did not challenge the redaction of the affidavit. The LSUC sought and received an order that the unredacted affidavit not be public to protect that privilege. The tribunal stated, at paragraph 5 of the decision, "We have assumed that privilege exists in the circumstances."

You can increase the likelihood that you, as a paralegal, will be able to claim privilege with regard to client communications by noting a claim to such privilege on documents, including email communications. When requesting information from clients or others, you should note that the request is being made for the purposes of providing legal advice. Similarly, in reply emails or letters, you should indicate that the communication is being made in response to a request for legal advice. You should, of course, maintain a professional tone in all communications.

Avoid Inadvertent Disclosure of Confidential Information

For most legal services providers, the major pitfall with regard to disclosure of confidential client communications or information is not deliberate disclosure, but inadvertent disclosure. Paragraph 19 of Guideline 8 of the *Paralegal Professional*

---

1 Law Society of Upper Canada, *Paralegal Rules of Conduct* (1 October 2014; amendments current to 2017), online: <https://www.lsuc.on.ca/paralegal-conduct-rules>.

2 (2007), 86 OR (3d) 612 (Sup Ct J).

Conduct Guidelines,[3] which supplements Rule 3.03(1) regarding confidentiality, provides steps to help you protect confidential client information. You should

- not disclose having been consulted or been retained by a particular person unless the nature of the matter requires disclosure;
- not disclose to one client confidential information about another client, and decline any retainer that would require such disclosure;
- avoid indiscreet conversations about your clients' affairs with others, including your spouse or family;
- not gossip about client affairs, even when the gossip does not involve naming or otherwise identifying the client;
- not repeat gossip or information about a client's business or affairs that you overhear or that is recounted to you; and
- avoid taking part in or listening to indiscreet "shop talk" between colleagues that may be overheard by third parties.

It is important that you think carefully before engaging in seemingly innocent conversation that may in fact be a breach of confidentiality, especially if you know clients on a personal basis or have common acquaintances—for example, if your client was referred to you by another client.

Permitted Disclosure of Confidential Information

Chapter 6 lists several situations in which paralegals are permitted to disclose confidential information. Section 9 of Guideline 8 provides that where a paralegal is retained to represent a client in a Small Claims Court action, the paralegal has the client's implied authority to disclose enough information about the client to complete the necessary court forms. Those forms generally ask for the client's address, phone number, and fax number (if the client has a fax number). Disclosure of this information does not breach Rule 3.03(1), although many paralegals prefer to leave that portion of the court form blank, noting that the client can be contacted via the paralegal's business address.

Protecting Confidential Information: Office Procedures

Referencing Rule 3.03(1) and (3) and Rule 8.01(1), paragraph 20 of Guideline 8 also recommends office procedures that can help you protect the confidentiality of clients and avoid conflicts of interest. You should do the following:

- Record identifying information and particulars about every client or potential client. A useful way of doing this is to take basic information before making an appointment to see the client.

---

3 Law Society of Upper Canada, *Paralegal Professional Conduct Guidelines* (1 October 2014; amendments current to 2017), online: <http://www.lsuc.on.ca/paralegal-conduct-guidelines>.

- Screen for conflicts of interest at the first contact with a client, using the identifying information you recorded. You should do this before you give the client any advice and before the client discloses any confidential information to you.

- Establish with each client a communication policy in which you outline how communications will be conducted. Are electronic communications acceptable? What is the client's preferred contact telephone number? Can messages be left at a home telephone number? Where should letters be sent?

- Set up your office in such a way that client files, file cabinets, and computers cannot be seen and/or accessed by non-employees. Be sure to shred confidential information before discarding it, and ensure appropriate security for off-site storage of files.

- Take steps to protect confidential information obtained and sent in electronic form.

- Train and supervise all staff to ensure they understand their obligations with respect to confidentiality.

- Limit access to confidential information by outside service providers. For example, if you contract business evaluators, accountants, or lawyers for services on a particular file, you should only provide them with the information they require to complete their tasks.

Once you have office procedures in place, ensure that they are followed consistently, even when things get hectic.

Systems and Tools for Managing Client Files

The LSUC's *Practice Management Guidelines*[4] were written to help lawyers assess, maintain, and enhance the quality of their services, but the framework they provide for conducting various aspects of legal work will also help paralegals meet their professional obligations and ensure compliance with the Rules.

Professionalism mandates—and Guideline 3.5 of the *File Management Practice Management Guideline* recommends—the creation, collection, and maintenance of the following in managing client files:

- databanks of key information regarding current and former clients, including
  - clients' names, aliases, and former names,
  - the dates that files were opened and/or closed, and
  - the subject matter of each file;
- information regarding conflicting or adverse parties, including
  - names of persons related to, or associated with, a client or former client, or the names of persons relevant to client or former client matters, and
  - cross references to the client or former client file name, file number, and matter reference;

---

4 Law Society of Upper Canada, *Practice Management Guidelines* (2009; amendments current to 2016), online: <http://www.lsuc.on.ca/For-Lawyers/Manage-Your-Practice/Representation/Client-Service/Practice-Management-Guidelines/>.

- information regarding billing and accounting; and
- information regarding key dates with reference to files, such as a tickler or other time management system.

Every time a client retains your services, a new client file should be opened, even if it contains only the date and time of a consultation. The file should be opened only after a conflict check has been performed and no conflict has been found. Each file should have its own folder. See Appendix 8.1 to this chapter for a file opening checklist produced by the LSUC that is for use by law firms but that can also be used by paralegal firms.

Various computer software programs such as PCLaw, Amicus Attorney, and Law-Stream can assist you in managing client files. Although client files are generally kept in hard copy, as more legal business is conducted online, it may be appropriate for you to have electronic files in certain situations. Whatever the format of your files, you must keep each file and its contents secure.

For a more comprehensive description and discussion of client file management practices, see *Working in a Legal Environment* by Collis and Forget.[5]

Tickler Systems and Checklists

In order to meet your obligations under the Rules—particularly Rule 3.01, which requires paralegals to perform all services undertaken on a client's behalf to the standard of a competent paralegal—it is important that you document all work to be done and dates of importance with regard to each client file (see also Guideline 6). Failure to take all necessary steps (such as drafting, serving, and filing of documents) or to remember the dates and times of events (such as court dates, meetings, limitation periods, and other deadlines) in relation to a particular matter may cause you to breach your professional obligations and may result in a claim of professional negligence against you.

Two important tools you should employ to manage and meet your obligations are tickler systems and checklists. **Ticklers** will provide you with advance notice of upcoming obligations and events. For example, you will want to be reminded of a deadline in advance of the last day for serving documents so that you have time to prepare them and serve them. You can also use your tickler system to manage other business-related obligations—for example, if utility bills are due on the first day of each month and rent is due on the last day, you can set these as recurring items on your tickler, noted a few days in advance so that those responsible have adequate time to arrange for payment.

A **checklist** is a list of things to be done or steps to be taken in relation to a file or other aspect of business management. Checklists can help you to stay organized, break tasks down into manageable chunks, and meet your professional obligations. They can also serve as a record of the fact that certain tasks were completed, and when. This can be useful in the event that you need to defend yourself against a claim of incompetence or negligence.

tickler
a system that is used to provide notice of future obligations and events, such as court dates, meetings, limitation periods, and other deadlines

checklist
a list of things to be done or steps to be taken in relation to a file or other aspect of business management

---

5   D Collis & C Forget, *Working in a Legal Environment* (Toronto: Emond Montgomery, 2007).

You can append a checklist to each client file to identify the steps you must take in relation to the file, for example, drafting, serving, and filing of certain documents. Depending on the matter and your type of practice, the contents of your checklists will differ. A checklist for a litigation matter, for example, might contain the following tasks:

- conduct initial client interview;
- ensure retainer arrangements are made, paid, and signed;
- confirm retainer with initial letter stating terms of engagement;
- instruct client regarding what to preserve in relation to the case;
- obtain copies of any statements made by a client;
- obtain copies of any court documents relating to the file;
- obtain copies of basic client documents;
- determine what fact gathering needs to be done; and
- note limitation periods, serving and filing deadlines, and deadlines and obligations with regard to discovery and/or disclosure.[6]

Computer software programs are used increasingly to ensure that deadlines and obligations are met. Many systems—such as the ones mentioned above—provide electronic checklists and tickler systems, which offer advantages over paper-based systems. Electronic systems can be used remotely via the Internet and can synchronize the calendars of various users, and data that is backed up or saved in electronic form can be stored more securely than notes written on paper.

Although they offer advantages, software systems can be quite expensive, and at the outset of your business, other programs—or even a paper desk calendar—will likely serve you adequately. You can access free calendars online (such as the ones made available by Google), and you can use less expensive calendar programs that are available with basic word-processing and office software. Many legal services professionals use devices such as BlackBerries and smartphones to set up their tickler systems and checklists.

Tickler systems for client service obligations and for business management can be kept separately or combined. The advantage of using one system is that you can use a single tool to view all of your obligations on a given date and immediately identify any scheduling conflicts. You may also wish to enter personal obligations into the same system.

Docketing

time docket
a record of time spent on billable and non-billable matters detailing work done, for how long, and on what matter

You will hear the term "docket" or "court docket" used to refer to a list of court cases or other matters scheduled over a particular day or other period of time, and assigned to a specified judge. In the context of practice management, a **time docket** is a record of time that was spent on billable and non-billable matters and that details the work that was done, on what matter, and how long it took to complete.

billable time
time that is charged to a client

Billable time is time that is charged to a client on an invoice, so it is important that you document this accurately. Most lawyers and many paralegals choose to charge

---

6   Based on material provided by the LSUC.

clients for time spent working on a file rather than use other methods, such as block fees for completion of specific tasks or contingency fees. The choice is yours, and you may choose to utilize a combination of methods. However, if you are charging for your time, you must keep track of it!

Non-billable time is time that is not billed to the client. This includes time spent on things such as professional development and continuing education, marketing, community service work, and business management. Documenting your non-billable time is important because it can help you determine which activities are inefficient or unproductive, and allow you to plan for future budgeting by calculating how much time must be spent on administrative and other business tasks. By monitoring your non-billable time, you may discover that you can operate a more profitable practice if you delegate such tasks to others, such as to an administrative assistant, a process server, a cleaning service, a bookkeeper, or an information technology specialist. Your time is usually better spent focusing on providing legal services for your clients.

Although you will seek to maximize billable time in order to ensure that the amount of money coming into your practice exceeds your expenses, both billable and non-billable time are crucial to the operation of a successful, ethical, and financially viable paralegal practice. In the long term, your practice and your reputation will be greatly enhanced by your ability to make appropriate use of non-billable time.

Software systems designed for use in the legal services industry often have complex docketing systems that allow for electronic record-keeping in nuanced ways. Many can provide statistical analysis of time spent in various capacities. This is useful for financial analysis and planning, and in determining appropriate compensation for employees. However, you may also docket by recording time spent on files in spreadsheets or on paper. Whatever method you choose, the key to effective docketing is recording your time consistently and promptly. You should have the docketing software or paper docket on your desktop, and you should docket throughout the business day rather than at the end of it. You will be surprised at how quickly you forget, especially if you are dealing with several matters throughout the day.

In the following scenario, an experienced paralegal gets behind with her docketing and cannot bill clients for work performed.

non-billable time
time that is not billed to the client, including time spent on things such as professional development and continuing education, marketing, community service work, and business management

PLANNING FOR PRACTICE

A Matter of Time

Candace Ling was accustomed to keeping a busy schedule. After obtaining her paralegal licence, she spent three years working in a high-profile, high-volume personal injury law firm. Not only was she responsible for managing a high volume of clients, but she was required by the demands of the partners to devote many hours to bringing in new clients and generating revenue for the firm.

All lawyers and paralegals were expected to network and follow up with previous clients whose matters had been resolved in order to gauge their satisfaction. This usually resulted in an opportunity to solicit referrals. Each member of the team was expected to bring in 10 to 15 new clients per month.

The firm's partners consistently praised Ling for bringing in new clients, many of whom were referred by clients who appreciated her skill and tenacious efforts on their behalf, getting them the best possible outcome.

Ling took leave from the firm when she became pregnant with her first child. During this time, she decided the schedule and demands of the firm did not suit her in her new role as parent.

Though the firm indicated she could work a more flexible schedule upon her return, she decided her best option was to start her own paralegal firm specializing in personal injury cases, working from home in the early years of the practice.

The skill of attracting clients she acquired from the previous firm served her well, and she was able to retain more than 70 clients in her first year.

In addition to managing cases for her clients, she diligently tended to all of the aspects of running her own business. Since she was not working for a large law firm, she did not have a team of legal assistants and accounting clerks to take care of more routine tasks such as filing, copying, scheduling, billing, and account collection. This now fell to her, with the help of a part-time legal assistant and her husband, who would occasionally pitch in.

After juggling the challenges of her new paralegal firm with those of raising a newborn daughter for a year, Ling started to feel overwhelmed by the amount of work she was putting in on a daily basis.

She found herself losing track of time and important aspects of her business. Though she was mostly on top of recording time spent working on client files, she missed some hours and could not bill them. From time to time she would fall behind in invoicing clients, which resulted in delayed payments for work she had performed. Time spent reaching out to and meeting prospective clients often went unrecorded and therefore she had no real sense of how much of her time this part of the business was taking.

Based on Ling's circumstances, what would you recommend she do to keep her business running smoothly so her work does not get in the way of her time with her daughter?

Organizing File Contents

Ultimately, how you organize your files is a combination of professional judgment and personal preference. What is most important is that you have systems in place, and that files are accessible and organized in a manner that makes them usable. Guideline 3.6.2 of the *File Management Practice Management Guideline* recommends that you employ systems that allow you to

- store and efficiently retrieve information about clients and opposing parties;
- open and maintain active client files;
- check for any potential conflicts;
- check for limitation periods that may affect the work to be done on a file;
- close, retain, and appropriately dispose of client files;

- review on an ongoing basis and, where necessary, change management systems to keep them effective and up to date;
- identify and place clients' property in safekeeping; and
- comply with the LSUC's bookkeeping and record-keeping requirements.

The file management section also suggests that it is often useful to organize client files into subfiles or subfolders that contain only a certain class or type of document. Depending on the type of file and the nature of the matter, you might have subfiles for

- communications (documentation of all telephone conversations and their details, any memos regarding client conversations and meetings, and copies of emails sent and received);
- research (including relevant case law, substantive research memoranda, and any investigations that have been done with respect to the file);
- original documents pertaining to the file (for example, a statement of claim in a civil litigation, or forms in an immigration matter);
- the retainer (including the signed retainer agreement as well as receipts for any moneys received);
- firm accounts and billing information;
- undertakings to be satisfied; and
- any other specific subfolders appropriate to the file.

Where possible, you should consider having an employee review client files periodically to ensure that their contents are organized efficiently and tidily, and that relevant dates are noted.

Regardless of the organization system that you choose to implement, for it to be effective you must ensure that it is followed.

Preserving Client Property

Property is a very broad concept. It can be defined as anything that is owned by an identifiable person or group of persons. It includes homes, land, and vehicles, as well as intellectual property—that is, ideas and inventions under copyright or trademark.

Rule 3.07 deals with client property, and the obligation of paralegals to preserve such property when it is entrusted to them. The term "**client property**" covers a wide range of items, such as money or other valuables, physical items, and information (Guideline 10); it includes retainer funds and any other funds or property given to you for safekeeping. Before accepting property to safeguard, you must satisfy yourself that you are able to keep it safe and that in doing so you will not inadvertently be participating in a crime—for example, by having stolen property or evidence in your possession. You may refuse to take client property into your possession if you have any concerns of this nature.

client property
property owned by the client, including money or other valuables, physical items, and information (Guideline 10), as well as retainer funds and any other funds or property given to a paralegal for safekeeping

As discussed in Chapter 7, according to section 18 of By-Law 9,[7] paralegals should maintain a **valuable property record** in order to document storage and delivery of client property. This may include stocks, bonds, or other securities in bearer form; jewellery, fur, paintings, collector's items, or any saleable valuables; and any other property that a paralegal could possibly convert into cash (Guideline 10). The valuable property record should not include items that cannot be sold or negotiated by the paralegal, for example, wills, securities registered in the name of the client, corporate seals, or records. These items should be listed carefully but separately from the valuable property record.

The valuable property record is an important tool for managing client property and may be useful should you need to defend yourself against complaints or claims made by clients.

Storing Active Files

Your office procedures must allow you to protect client confidentiality in accordance with Rule 3.03(1) and (3). Guideline 8 provides helpful advice regarding how to store active client files appropriately in order to ensure this.

First, you should physically position files in a way that is mindful of your confidentiality obligations. Client files must be kept out of sight. You should consider keeping filing cabinets in a discreet location away from the reception area and locking them when no one is in the office. Computer screens should be located and angled in such a way as to prevent people not in the firm (that is, non-employees) from viewing them, and you should consider using privacy screens for laptops. Finally, you should consider limiting access to particular client files to only those staff who are working on the matter, shredding confidential information before discarding it, and ensuring appropriate security for offsite storage of files.

You must also take appropriate steps to protect the confidentiality of client information in electronic form. This may include using firewall software, encrypting information, and using passwords where appropriate. If you are travelling with a laptop that contains client information, you should be particularly careful and should be advised that when crossing international borders your laptop may be subject to search and seizure or to a review of its files. Electronic data transfer over an encrypted communications channel—such as zipped files sent through email networks—may be a better means of transmitting client data.

Closing and Storing Inactive Client Files

When matters to which a client file relates are completed or if the client terminates the retainer, you must close the client file. Closed files should be kept separate from active files. Closed client files should be assigned codes and stored in an orderly, retrievable manner in a single location. Closed paper files can be sent to a secure,

---

7   Law Society of Upper Canada, By-Law 9 (1 May 2007; last amended 27 April 2017), online: <https://www.lsuc.on.ca/by-laws/>.

offsite storage location, while closed electronic files should be retained in a manner that allows them to be searchable and accessible.

Because your duty of confidentiality to your clients lasts indefinitely—including after a client's death—you must ensure that you protect your clients' confidentiality after the files become inactive. Client files must be closed, and confidential materials disposed of, carefully. Simply throwing closed files into a dumpster without shredding them first, for example, would be a potential breach of your duty.

The process of closing files should involve, first of all, a review of the file. All unnecessary items, such as first drafts of pleadings or correspondence, should be removed and individual documents returned to the appropriate parties. Documents that a client gives to you in the course of your professional relationship remain the property of the client, and the client should be provided with all such documents. Generally, documents that belong to the client include

- the client's original documents and photographs;
- originals or copies of documents prepared for the client;
- copies of documents for which the client has paid;
- the opposing party's documents;
- pleadings and court documents;
- expert reports; and
- copies of case law or legal memoranda where the client has paid for the research.[8]

Having the client sign an acknowledgment of receipt of the file contents upon closure of the file is good practice. In addition, when closing a file you should retain a copy of all documents returned to the client for your own records in the form of either paper copies or scanned documents. You will need these in the event that you are required to defend against a negligence claim or a complaint to the LSUC.

Conclusion

Unreserved communication between paralegals and their clients is essential for effective legal advice, and is facilitated by confidentiality. You should take steps to increase the likelihood that your communications with clients will be privileged, and you must avoid inadvertent disclosure of confidential information. Do not disclose confidential information about one client to another, or disclose having been consulted or retained by a particular person unless the nature of the matter requires it. Avoid indiscreet conversations about your clients' affairs, and do not partake in or repeat gossip related to a client's affairs.

Implement office procedures that allow you to protect client confidentiality and avoid conflicts of interest. Among other procedures, you might record identifying information and particulars about every client or potential client and use this to

---

8 Based on material provided by the LSUC.

screen for conflicts of interest; establish a communication policy with each client; set up your office and storage systems to protect confidentiality; take steps to protect confidential information obtained and sent in electronic form; train and supervise all staff to ensure they understand their obligations with respect to confidentiality; and limit access to confidential information by outside service providers.

You should open a new client file every time a client retains your services, even if the file contains only the date and time of a consultation. The file should be opened only after a conflict check has been performed and no conflict has been found. You must document all work to be done and dates of importance regarding client files. Checklists and tickler systems can help you meet your obligations in this area; the latter can also help you manage other business-related obligations, such as payment of bills. You may use electronic or paper-based systems, and may choose to keep checklists and tickler systems for client service obligations, business management, and personal obligations separate or to combine them in a single system.

If you charge for your time, you must use a time docket to keep track of billable and non-billable time. Both are crucial to the operation of a successful, ethical, and financially viable practice. As you seek to maximize your billable time, your ability to make appropriate use of non-billable time will greatly enhance your practice and your reputation in the long term.

To document storage and delivery of client property, you should maintain a valuable property record. If you have any concerns about the property a client is asking you to safeguard—for example, in accepting it you may be participating in a crime—you may refuse to take the property into your possession.

Employ a file organization system that allows you to store and efficiently retrieve information about clients and opposing parties; open and maintain active client files; screen for conflicts; check for limitation periods; close, retain, and appropriately dispose of client files; review and make changes to management systems to keep them effective and up to date; identify and place clients' property in safekeeping; and comply with the LSUC's bookkeeping and record-keeping requirements.

To protect client confidentiality, you should keep client files out of sight. Consider keeping filing cabinets away from the reception area and locking them when no one is in the office, and limiting access to particular client files to only those staff who are working on the matter. Locate and angle computer screens so that non-employees cannot view them, and use privacy screens for laptops. Shred confidential information before discarding it, and ensure appropriate security for offsite storage of files.

When closing a file, return to the client any documents that belong to the client, and have the client sign an acknowledgment of receipt of the file contents. Keep scanned copies or photocopies of all documents in the file for your records. Store closed paper and electronic client files in an orderly, retrievable manner in a single location.

APPENDIX 8.1

File Opening Checklist

FILE OPENING CHECKLIST

Client(s): ▓▓▓▓▓▓▓   File No: ▓▓▓▓▓▓   ✓ entered into accounting/docketing system

CRUCIAL DATE

Date: ▓▓▓▓▓▓▓▓▓▓▓▓▓▓▓
(DD MM YY)

✓ Recorded in bring forward system

Required Action: ▓▓▓▓▓▓▓▓▓▓▓

Action completed on: ▓▓▓▓▓▓▓▓▓▓▓
(DD/MM/YY)

-OR-
▓ N/A, Explain: ▓▓▓▓▓▓▓▓▓▓▓

CLIENT(S) CONTACT INFORMATION

Name(s) ▓▓▓▓▓▓▓▓▓▓▓

Address ▓▓▓▓▓▓▓▓▓▓▓

Telephone ▓▓▓▓▓▓▓▓▓▓▓

Cell ▓▓▓▓▓▓▓▓▓▓▓

Email ▓▓▓▓▓▓▓▓▓▓▓

Name of instructing individual (if Institution): ▓▓▓▓▓▓▓▓

Special instructions re: client communications: ▓▓▓▓▓▓

MATTER/PARTIES

Brief Description: ▓▓▓▓▓▓▓▓▓

Name of Opposing Party(ies): ▓▓▓▓▓▓▓▓

Opposing Party/Lawyer/Paralegal Information

Name ▓▓▓▓▓▓▓▓▓▓▓

Address ▓▓▓▓▓▓▓▓▓▓▓

Telephone ▓▓▓▓▓▓▓▓▓▓▓

Cell ▓▓▓▓▓▓▓▓▓▓▓

Email ▓▓▓▓▓▓▓▓▓▓▓

Cross-Reference Location:

Electronic file documents: █████████████████████

Bankers boxes: █████████████████████

Client Property (wills, minute books, key evidence, etc.): ███████████

███████████████████████████

FILE MANAGEMENT/SYSTEMS REQUIREMENTS

✓ *(check when complete)*

▨ First bring forward date recorded in bring forward/tickler system

▨ Results of conflicts search reviewed/assessed by lawyer/paralegal:
  Initials: ██████████████   Date: █████████████
  Location of conflict search results:

Written confirmation of retainer in file
▨ copy of confirming email/letter   **-OR-**   ▨ signed retainer agreement

Is this a joint retainer?
▨ No   ▨ Yes
        ▨ Written confirmation of consents (to joint retainer) by all joint clients in file

▨ Client ID obtained   **-OR-**   ▨ Exemption applies

Location of ID recordsor memo to file explaining exemption:

In this matter, will lawyer/paralegal be engaged in or give instructions respecting the receiving, paying, or transferring of funds?
▨ No   ▨ Yes
        ▨ Client verification is required   **-OR-**   ▨ Exemption applies

Location of verification records or memo to file explaining exemption:
Has there/will there be a receipt of trust funds?
▨ No   ▨ Yes
        ▨ Purpose of **each** receipt of funds into trust identified **and** recorded in firm's books and records

---

* The "File Opening Checklist" provided at Appendix 8.1 is based on information provided in the Law Society's "File Opening Checklist." It is not a form produced by, or approved by, The Law Society of Upper Canada.

KEY TERMS

billable time, 122
checklist, 121
client property, 125
non-billable time, 123
solicitor–client privilege, 118
tickler, 121
time docket, 122
valuable property record, 126

USEFUL URLS

Farcht, Joe. "A Checklist for an Efficient Home Office
Work Area." <http://www.homeofficeweekly.com/
office-space/efficient-work-area.html>.

Legaltech News. <http://www.legaltechnews.com>.

Perman, Matt. 2009. "A Few Quick Examples on How
to Make Your Tickler File Electronic." <https://
www.whatsbestnext.com/2009/03/a-few-quick
-examples-on-how-to-make-your-tickler-file
-electronic/>.

REVIEW QUESTIONS

1. How can paralegals avoid inadvertent disclosure of
   confidential information?

2. What are some office procedures that paralegals
   can employ to prevent breaches of confidentiality?

3. What is a tickler system?

4. What is a checklist, and what functions does it
   serve?

5. What is a time docket, and why is it useful?

6. When deciding how to organize client files, what
   must paralegals ensure that their systems allow
   them to do?

7. What must a paralegal do when matters to which a
   client file relates are completed or when the client
   terminates the retainer?

8. Explain how inactive or closed client files should be
   stored.

9. If a paralegal spends one hour drafting an
   advertisement for her practice, is that time billable
   or non-billable time?

10. If a paralegal spends two hours conducting legal
    research in order to prepare for a sentencing
    hearing in a *Highway Traffic Act* matter, is that time
    billable or non-billable time?

SCENARIO-BASED QUESTIONS

1. **Making Demands**

   Gurpreet Sandhu is a paralegal. He works for the
   large law firm Bell, Hook, and Smee LLP. Five days
   ago Gurpreet Sandhu accepted a retainer in a small
   claims matter representing the plaintiff, Ann Peters.
   Before accepting the retainer, he conducted a
   conflicts check, which came back clear. His first
   action on the file was to send a demand letter to
   the defendant John Michaels, outlining the cause of
   action and seeking payment of the sum of $8,000.
   The letter stated that if the payment was not made,
   a Small Claims Court action would be commenced.
   John Michaels receives the letter and is very angry.
   He telephones Gurpreet and says: "Why is my own
   law firm sending me a letter threatening to sue
   me?" Apparently, John Michaels is the sole
   shareholder, president, and director of a
   corporation, 113456 Ontario Inc. carrying on
   business as JM Foods. Bell, Hook, and Smee LLP has
   represented that corporation for ten years, though,
   in his three years at the firm, Gurpreet Sandhu has
   never worked on a file for JM Foods. John Michaels
   tells Gurpreet that he will be finding another law
   firm to represent the corporation. When Gurpreet
   investigates the matter he realizes that his conflicts
   check was sent out under the name John Michael
   rather than John Michaels, which is why the
   conflicts check came back clear. Had the conflict
   check been conducted under the proper name, it
   would have revealed that John Michaels was the
   director and President of 113456 Ontario Inc.
   carrying on business as JM Foods. Although
   corporations are separate legal entities from their
   shareholders, Bell, Hook, and Smee LLP is careful to

list the principals of corporations so that it can avoid precisely this kind of embarrassing incident.

a. Is Bell, Hook, and Smee LLP required to list the principals of its corporate clients? Explain your answer citing any relevant Rules and Guidelines.

b. What does Gurpreet need to tell Ann Peters?

2. Sloppy Sam

Sam Speight's desk is covered with client files, his in-tray is full of loose pieces of paper that need to be filed in those files, and the three chairs in his office are piled high with client files. Sam likes to work in what he calls "controlled chaos" and has instructed the office building's cleaners not to disturb anything on his desk or chair when they come in to empty his garbage and recycling bins. He is careful to shred confidential material and is also careful never to meet clients in his office. Instead he meets them in the office's conference room, which is always kept clear of papers except for those he needs to discuss with the particular client with whom he is meeting. Sam is certain that he has fulfilled his obligation to preserve client confidentiality. Has he?

Glossary

advertising efforts to draw attention to a product or a business in order to encourage sales, generally through paid announcements in various media

articles of incorporation a document filed with the appropriate government authority that provides for incorporation as of right, provided that the required steps are followed

asset item of value owned by a company or person, including tangible items such as buildings and equipment, and intangible ones such as telephone numbers and licences

asset sale a sale in which a business's tangible assets are sold, but not its name, corporate identity, work in progress, and goodwill

bankruptcy a legal process governed by the *Bankruptcy and Insolvency Act* for a person who can no longer pay back debt; the person who owes the debt assigns all assets—with some exceptions—to a Licensed Insolvency Trustee who sells it or uses it to help pay the debt to the creditors

billable time time that is charged to a client

budget a list of anticipated income and expenses for a defined future period

business communication communication for the purpose of carrying out business activities; includes marketing, customer relations, branding, community engagement, advertising, public relations, and employee management

business plan a document that contains a summary of a business's operational and financial objectives, along with detailed plans and budgets that explain how the objectives will be achieved

cash flow movement of money into and out of a business

certificate of authorization a certificate issued by the LSUC that permits a corporation to provide legal services

checklist a list of things to be done or steps to be taken in relation to a file or other aspect of business management

client a person who (a) consults a paralegal and on whose behalf the paralegal provides or agrees to provide legal services, or (b) having consulted the paralegal, reasonably concludes that the paralegal has agreed to act on his or her behalf; includes a client of the firm of which the paralegal is a partner or associate, whether or not the paralegal handles the client's work (Rule 1.02)

client profile data relating to the demographics of a business's potential clients—such as their geographic location, age, income level, gender, ethnicity, and education level—that allows business owners to assess the needs of their target market

client property property owned by the client, including money or other valuables, physical items, and information (Guideline 10), as well as retainer funds and any other funds or property given to a paralegal for safekeeping

competent paralegal a paralegal who has and applies the relevant skills, attributes, and values appropriate to each matter undertaken on a client's behalf (Rule 3.01(4))

confidential information any information that paralegals gain in the course of their professional relationship with a client; paralegals have a duty to hold all such information in strict confidence indefinitely and may not disclose it to any other person, unless authorized to do so by the client or required to do so by law (Rule 3.03(1))

conflict of interest the existence of a substantial risk that a paralegal's loyalty to or representation of a client would be materially and adversely affected by the paralegal's own interest or the paralegal's duties to another client, a former client, or a third person; the risk must be more than a mere possibility; there must be a genuine, serious risk to the duty of loyalty or to client representation arising from the retainer

contingency fee a fee paid based on a percentage of the final settlement or judgment, and therefore payable only if the client is successful

corporation a business entity that has a legal existence separate and apart from that of the individuals who created it or who operate it

delegate to assign tasks to others

due diligence investigation of a business or a person, or the performance of an act to ensure compliance with legal or other standards

entrepreneur an individual who starts up a new business

errors and omissions insurance the insurance that covers an individual licensee in the event that a client is successful in suing for professional negligence; also called professional liability insurance

ethics a branch of philosophy that seeks to address questions about morality; a codified set of moral rules specific to the performance of professional obligations

fee splitting occurs when a paralegal shares or divides his or her fee with another person

fiduciary duty an obligation, with respect to financial matters, to put the interests of the person owed the duty above one's own interests

financial analysis a business's comparison of its budgeted numbers with actual numbers to find explanations for differences between its anticipated and actual earnings and expenses, and to help it determine things such as whether it is setting appropriate fees and renting suitable office space

financial plan a key component of a business plan that concerns the money coming into and going out of the business; shows how much money is required to operate the business and where that money is coming from

franchise a licence granting the right to use trademarks, trade names, business methods, and systems for products and services

franchisee the one to whom the licence is granted

franchisor the one who grants the licence

general account a firm's operating account that contains money belonging to the firm; funds held in that account will be used to pay bills owed by the firm

goodwill an intangible asset consisting of a business's reputation and brand, measured by the difference in the value of its assets (minus liabilities) and the market value of the company

independent legal advice/independent legal representation legal advice provided by a legal representative to represent the interests of a person or organization who requires legal service from a different legal services provider because of a conflict of interest that prevents the paralegal who was originally consulted from giving advice to the person or organization

insolvency the inability of a debtor to pay debt as it is due

joint and several liability shared liability, such that all parties are equally liable for the full amount of the debt or obligation

Law Society of Upper Canada (LSUC) a professional organization that governs legal services in Ontario with a mandate to ensure that the people of Ontario are served by lawyers and paralegals who set standards of education, competence, and conduct

legal services services that involve applying legal principles and legal judgment to the circumstances and objectives of a client

liabilities debts and other financial obligations

limited liability partnership a partnership of professionals where not all of the partners are liable for the professional negligence of one or some of the partners

limited partnership a type of partnership that restricts liability to only one or some of the partners, as set out in a partnership agreement

management plan the part of a business plan that outlines how the business is structured and describes the responsibilities of various individuals with respect to its management

market analysis used by business owners, in the planning stages of their business and on an ongoing basis, to help them determine the opportunities and risks of a particular market and how these may affect their success

market profile a business tool, created through research, that provides business owners with important information about areas of opportunity in the market—for example, common legal problems in a particular market

marketing a broader concept than advertising that focuses on branding, such as with the use of letterhead, business cards, and logos (Rule 8.03)

marketing plan a document that sets out actions identified as necessary for a business to achieve its marketing objectives

multi-discipline partnership a partnership of licensees and other professionals, such as account-ants and tax consultants, through which paralegals can provide their clients with non-legal professional services that support the provision of legal services

multi-discipline practice (MDP) Lawyers and licensed paralegals may form a Multi-Discipline Practice with professionals who practise a profession, trade, or occupation that supports or supplements their practise of law or provision of legal service (e.g., accountants, tax consultants, trademark and patent agents, etc.)

non-billable time time that is not billed to the client, including time spent on things such as professional development and continuing education, marketing, community service work, and business management

non-engagement letter a letter from the paralegal or paralegal firm to someone who has consulted that paralegal or paralegal firm that clearly indicates that the paralegal or paralegal firm has not been retained in the matter that was the subject of the consultation

NUANS (Newly Upgraded Automated Name Search) a type of search that checks the name of the proposed business against business names that are already being used; trademarks are also checked

paralegal an individual who provides legal services and representation in permitted practice areas, and who has a licence to do so issued by the LSUC

partnership a form of business in which two or more persons carry on business together with a reasonable expectation of a profit; also called a general partnership

phantom client someone who believes that he or she is represented by a paralegal even though he or she has not formally retained or hired that paralegal

professional a member of a vocation founded upon specialized education and training and subject to standards of competence and ethics

professional corporation a corporation that protects shareholder-owners against personal liability but not against professional liability; must be authorized by the LSUC

professional responsibility refers to paralegals' obligations to observe the rules and ethics of the paralegal profession as determined by the LSUC

Professionalism Hours hours of continuing professional development covering topics such as ethics, professional responsibility, and/or practice management

referral agreement a signed written agreement between the referring paralegal or lawyer, the licensee to whom the client is referred, and the client being referred; the agreement must be in the form provided by the LSUC

referral fee a fee paid by a paralegal to another paralegal or lawyer for referring a client to the paralegal, or a fee paid to the paralegal by another paralegal or lawyer for his or her referral of a person to another paralegal or lawyer

retainer the advance payment made by a client, usually at the time that the retainer agreement is signed, that is deposited in the paralegal's trust account

retainer agreement a contract between two parties through which one pays to reserve the time of the other and secures the performance of professional services

retainer letter a letter from the paralegal or paralegal firm to the client; the letter confirms the existence of a retainer, the scope of that retainer, and generally contains the same information as a retainer agreement, but is not signed by the client

sole proprietorship a business owned by a single individual, where there is no legal distinction between the owner of the business and the business itself

solicitor–client privilege privilege extended to communications between lawyers and their clients where legal advice is sought or provided and when the parties to the communication intend that information to be confidential; the concept of privilege means that the lawyer cannot be compelled to disclose the information as evidence; privilege belongs to the client

standard of care the level of care, competence, or prudence required to avoid liability for negligence

strategic planning the process of assessing the current business situation and the environment to determine whether they are changing, and revising the business plans to reflect the findings

Substantive Hours hours of continuing professional development that generally deal with topics such as developments in various areas of law, particular skills, and/or practice and procedure

SWOT analysis an analysis of strengths, weaknesses, opportunities, and threats; it may be used when considering competition, changes in technology, changes in regulation, or the scope of a paralegal's practice

tickler a system that is used to provide notice of future obligations and events, such as court dates, meetings, limitation periods, and other deadlines

time docket a record of time spent on billable and non-billable matters detailing work done, for how long, and on what matter

transaction with a client a transaction to which a paralegal and a client of the paralegal are parties, whether or not other persons are also parties; includes lending or borrowing money, buying or selling property or services having other than nominal value, giving or acquiring ownership, security, or other pecuniary interest in a company or other entity, recommending an investment, or entering into a common business venture

trust account a separate account that paralegals must maintain to keep client funds held in trust

valuable property record a written record that documents the paralegal's receipt, storage, and delivery of all client property other than trust funds

Index